Table of Contents

Introduction

Parents always want to grow their children into healthy and emotionally intelligent individuals. They want their kids to earn a good reputation and achieve success in their life. There are ways to strengthen parent-child bonds and get a win-win result, but positive parenting is the top most skill that helps parent-kid bonding. Parents are worried about their kids; they want to keep them happy and stay satisfied. Adopting positive parenting techniques will help you become a successful parent.

There are different parenting styles people use according to their temperament. These parenting styles include authoritative, authoritarian, permissive, and un-involved style of parenting. From these styles, authoritative parenting styles help a parent as it has some freedom but has some boundaries. It tends to result in happy, capable, and effective kids.

Being a parent, you may have many expectations from your kids, but sometimes it makes things difficult to handle for the kid, and he is so nervous that he cannot meet the goals. Do not set high expectations from your kids; instead, appreciate their efforts regardless of results. Enjoy the journey with your children towards a target, show them attention, and give your time to listen to them. Instead of punishing your child, choose to be a calm parent, and make your kids understand what you want to communicate politely. It will decrease the whining nature of kids.

Kids are more prone to show stress for their small tasks, and they are stressed because they are acing new things in their life. Being a parent, you can easily manage their stress by understanding their emotions and letting them face any fear that comes in their way. There are numerous ways you can choose to help your kids in this regard. Keep your kids safe from molesters by sharing information about how to keep themselves protected and how to ask others help from others if needed.

Confident and emotionally intelligent kids grow into healthy and productive human beings. But some kids lack confidence because of many reasons. Kids lack confidence due to parents' negligence or due to some trauma, mood changes, poor influencers in their company, or continuous medical conditions. Parents can help their kids overcome low self-esteem and polish their communication skills and make them good speakers.

Either you are a parent of an infant, toddler, or teen, the tips are available to happily manage your relationship with the child and make your kids super humans. In the later chapters of the guide, you will find a bundle of tips for different age groups from infants to teenagers. These tips will help you taking care of your kids' sleep, food, health, behavioral management, and safety as a priority.

Choose positive parenting and apply the tips for it, and you can be a happy parent with an emotionally intelligent individual.

Chapter 1: Concepts about Parent-Child Relationship

To ensure their safe growth into adulthood, the process of raising children, and providing them with security and care. Three main priorities are shared by parenting activities worldwide, ensuring children's health and well-being, preparing children for life as responsible adults, and transmitting cultural values. For healthy growth, a high-quality parent-child relationship is essential.

Parents exert incredible influence over their children's lives, from promoting schoolwork and sports to modeling principles as children develop (remember, they do as you do, not as you say!). However, they are not the only influencers on the ground, particularly after kids reach school and start engaging with the world at large.

Most parents work to give kids the best possible start, but it's also crucial for parents to remember that kids come into the world with their temperaments, attitudes, and ambitions. While parents may want to drive their child down a particular path, a parent's role is to provide an interaction with the world that eventually prepares a child for full independence and the freedom to follow whatever way they like.

Parenting can be subject to trends and evolving styles in a continually shifting environment, and parenting has become a competitive sport in some privileged circles. However, as outlined by science, child development needs remain reasonably stable: protection, structure, encouragement, and love.

1.1 Parenting and Child Development

As they age, developmental activities most important to children's change. A significant developmental challenge for an infant, for example, is attachment, while individualization is a popular activity for a toddler. Parenting during infancy and adolescence is at its highest degree of stress.

Children focus entirely on their caregivers in the first few years of life, who decide much of children's experiences. For example, caregivers determine whether a child is kept, spoken to, or ignored, and what kinds of activities the toddler can participate in. This time provides unprecedented opportunities for learning and growth, which are best enabled by an enhanced but not stressed environment because of the human nervous system's tremendous versatility during the early years.

Furthermore, while some researchers claim that later experiences can entirely change children's developmental processes, many argue that the experiences lay the framework on which the rest of development builds over the first few years of life. The caregiver's sensitivity to the signs of the child helps the child learn simple regulations and predicts the protection of the child's attachment to the caregiver, which is coordinated towards the end of the first year.

Parenting focuses on providing care, preferably from a warm and attentive caregiver, in the first few months of life. The sensitivity of the caregiver to the signs of the child helps the child learn simple regulations and predicts the protection of the attachment of the child to the caregiver, which is coordinated towards the end of the first year. The completely dependent infant becomes a passionately independent child in the second year of life, welcoming growing opportunities for discipline. When kids step further out into the world, early and middle childhood brings new challenges. School adaptation and peer relationships are central, and parents who are active and encouraging often help children here.

Adolescence, once described as a "storm and tension" phase, is now seen as a phase of dynamic transition, but one that is successfully navigated by most children (75-80 percent). Once upon a time, this era was often identified by the severing of relations between parents and their children.

Contemporary studies, however, show that even as they progress towards greater freedom, teenagers benefit from maintaining close and linked relationships with their parents. An expert in adolescent growth, the American psychiatrist Lynn Ponton, observed that risk taking is a natural part of the essential experimentation in which adolescents participate. By inspiring their kids to take constructive chances, such as trying out for a sports team, racing for a spot in the student government, or working on a special project, parents play a vital role. Adolescents participating in difficult but positive efforts, such as alcohol and substance use, are less likely to be attracted to negative risk taking.

1.2 Significance of Positive Parent for Child Development

The long-standing idea that, through the mechanism of socialization, parents have a direct and influential effect on their children has pervaded science and philosophy on human development and most systems of cultural belief. It is the parents' benefit if kids turn out well; if they turn out poorly, it is the parents' fault.

Researchers who stress the effect of biological factors on the development of children have questioned this assumption. For example, developmental genetic tests suggest that adopted children are more like their biological parents in essential characteristics such as personality, intelligence, and mental health than their adoptive parents. Besides, some scholars have criticized the focus on parenting by arguing that other variables, such as peer relationships, strongly influence development.

Several concerns are emphasized by scholars who study the importance of parenting. First, genetic and socialization factors are hard to distinguish in biologically related families. A musically talented child, for instance, may have inherited the trend from parents who are also musically gifted. Music at home is likely to be stressed by the same parents, making it difficult to decide whether the musical child results from biology, the setting, or (most likely) both of them working together. If the child has been adopted instead and is raised by parents who are not musically inclined, the talent's expression may take a different form or maybe be actively suppressed. Genetic predispositions (strengths and vulnerabilities) are, therefore, also altered by parent-created experiences.

Second, bidirectional rather than unidirectional is the stream of control between parents and children. An impatient parent may cause an infant to respond with distress, but the parent may evoke impatience from an infant who is constitutionally prone to pain. Parents and children frequently become trapped in escalating cycles of action and reaction, in this case, anxiety, and impatience, regardless of who has initiated the chain of events. However, since parents are more mature and experienced than children, they play a more significant role in developing the initial interaction patterns. They can trigger change more effectively by modifying their responses (e.g., reacting to the upset child with patience).

Finally, parents play an essential role in influencing children's environments and, therefore, the exposure of children to other influences that affect development, such as peer relationships. For example, parents are often more likely to make choices about the community in which the family lives, the schools in which children attend, and many of the events in which children participate; in this way, parents expose children to those peers, not others. Besides, kids are more likely to choose peers with shared preferences and beliefs, which are primarily rooted in early family interactions. Also, large factors of background, such as poverty and culture, are mediated by parents, who, in the words of American Psychologist Marc Bornstein, are the "final common pathway to the development and stature, adaptation and achievement of children."

1.3 What are the Different Parenting Styles?

One of the essentials about being a parent is that how we educate our children varies greatly. At the same time, from one parent to another, there are several parallels. Researchers have tried to group parents into four different parenting styles with appropriate similarity. Your style of parenting refers to the blend of techniques you use to raise your kids. One frequently cited Diane Baumrind 's work created the categorization of parenting styles in the 1960s. She established several essential aspects of parenting using naturalistic observation, parental interviews, and other research methods.

Disciplinary methods, comfort and nurturing, contact styles, and competence and control standards are included in these dimensions. Based on these dimensions, Baumrind proposed that most parents exhibit one of three distinct parenting types. Maccoby and Martin's later research proposed introducing a fourth type of parenting. Each of these has varying effects on the actions of children.

There are distinct names and features of the four Baumrind parenting styles:

- Authoritarian or Disciplinarian
- Permissive or Indulgent
- Uninvolved
- Authoritative

- **Authoritarian**

Children are supposed to obey the strict rules defined by parents in this style of parenting. Typically, failure to follow specific regulations results in a penalty. Authoritarian parents do not give explanations of the logic behind these laws. If the parent is asked to explain, he might respond, "Because I said so."

Although these parents have high expectations, their kids are not very receptive to them. They expect their kids to act outstandingly and not make mistakes, but they have very little advice about what their kids can do or avoid in the future. Mistakes are punished, often very severely, and their kids are often left questioning just what they have done wrong.

Baumrind notes that these parents are "obedience-oriented and status-oriented, and expect to follow their orders without explanation." They are also characterized as dictatorial and dominant. They believe that if you do not punish the child for his mistakes, he will not learn. Without a doubt, they expect children to follow.

- **Authoritative Parenting Style:**

Like authoritarian parents, parents with an authoritative parenting style set rules and guidelines that their children are supposed to follow. This parenting style is also more democratic, however.

Authoritative parents are sensitive and able to listen to questions about their kids. These parents expected a lot of their kids, but they provide comfort, feedback, and sufficient support. These parents are more nurturing and accommodating rather than punitive when children fail to meet standards.

Baumrind suggests that these parents track and impart consistent expectations for the actions of their children. They are assertive, but not disruptive and restrictive. Rather than punitive, their disciplinary practices are constructive. They want their children to be proactive and socially responsible, and self-regulated and cooperative.

- **Permissive Parents:**

Permissive parents demand significantly less from their children, often referred to as indulgent parents. Since they have relatively low standards of maturity and self-control, these parents rarely control their kids.

Permissive parents are more sensitive than they are demanding, according to Baumrind. They are non-traditional and lenient, do not require mature behavior, promote substantial self-regulation, and prevent conflict. Permissive parents usually nurture and interact with their children, often taking on a friend's status more than parents.

- **Uninvolved Parents:**

Psychologists Eleanor Maccoby and John Martin suggested a fourth style, in addition to the three primary styles proposed by Baumrind: uninvolved or neglectful parenting. There are few demands, low responsiveness, and minimal contact that define an uninvolved parenting style. While these parents meet the infant's basic needs, they are usually disconnected from the life of their infant. They might ensure that their children are fed and protected, but in the way of instruction, structure, laws, or even encouragement, they give little to nothing. These parents can also deny or ignore their children's needs in severe cases.

1.4 What is the Impact of Parenting Styles on Kids?

What impact do these parenting styles have on the outcome of child development? In addition to Baumrind 's initial study of 100 preschool children, various studies on the impact of parenting styles on children have been performed by researchers.

Among the results:

- Authoritarian parenting forms typically lead to obedient and capable children, but they rank lower in satisfaction, social skill, and self-esteem.

- Authoritative styles of parenting tend to result in happy, capable, and effective kids.

- Permissive parenting also results in children with low satisfaction and self-regulation rankings. Such kids are more likely to encounter authority issues and appear to do poorly in school.

- The uninvolved style of parenting ranks lowest in all spheres of life. Such kids tend to lack self-control, have low self-esteem, and are less professional than their colleagues.

- **Advantages of Authoritative Parenting**

Since authoritative parents are more likely to be considered rational, fair, and just, their kids will comply with their parents' requests. Often, kids are much more likely to internalize these lessons because they have rules and reasons for these rules. Instead of only following the rules because they are afraid of punishment (as they may be with authoritarian parents), the kids of authoritative parents will see why the rules exist. These kids understand that they are reasonable and appropriate, and aspire to obey them to satisfy their own internalized sense of right and wrong.

When both parents follow the same parenting style, it is simpler for the family; some research suggests that if at least one parent is authoritative, it is better for the child than having two parents do the same, less efficient style. And there are more factors on how children become, of course than just the type of parenting.

These components include some of the several other factors influencing the development of a child:

- The nature of the child and how it "fits" with the parents
- A method of interacting with children by teachers and a match between the teaching style and the parenting style
- The impact of the peer group of a child

New names for parenting styles are emerging today. For instance, "helicopter parenting" is similar to the authoritative style, but with a little more interest in children's lives, or some may say over-involvement. Free-range parenting "is similar to the uninvolved model, but with a deliberate decision to encourage the child to think more independently in the best interest."

It can be useful to focus on where you fit into the parenting style continuum. Taking it one step further: understand that at any point in time, any of us with any style might benefit from the self-reflection that usually comes from engaging in a parenting class. It can be helpful and encouraging to talk with other parents and a facilitator.

Chapter 2: How to Be a Positive Parent

Positive parenting is not about a permissive parenting style, which is highly sensitive and lowly demanding parenting. There is an emphasis on discipline through positive parenting, and the aim is to raise a child who follows the rules and respects others, not out of fear, but because it's the right thing to do.

2.1 What are the Ways to Be a Positive Parent?

We should all agree that parenting is a challenge, whether you are the parent of a baby or a teenager! One day can be fantastic, and then the next can be exhausting, frustrating, and overwhelming.

- How can I help my baby to sleep all night long?
- Why is my toddler not going to stop throwing toys?
- How am I going to make my teenage daughter stop talking back?

We still look for ways to improve our children; to make our children fit into a mold that works for us. However, this technique rarely works, and we face screaming babies, tantrums of toddlers, and sassy teens. What if we had stopped trying to change our children and changed ourselves instead? What if we altered our parenting styles and philosophies of parenting? What if through rose-colored lenses, we wanted to see parenting? What if we were to try not to take it all too seriously?

We can shift our thoughts and emotions about parenting challenges and become calmer and more optimistic parents. We'll probably enjoy our kids more by making a few little adjustments, and better yet, our children's habits will follow our lead. Here are a few minor improvements that will give your children a better and more positive relationship.

- **Set Some Boundaries.**

It is crucial to being productive in positive parenting to have limits in our relationship with our children. Having boundaries and following them helps us to be patient and calm because we feel respected and that our relationship needs are met. An excellent way to know when a new boundary needs to be formed is when a repeated action or circumstance makes you feel exasperated, impatient, or angry.

Are you afraid of dinner time because your kid demands that you sit on his lap and you can't eat? If so, create a rule that everyone sits for meals in their chair. After supper, you should snuggle. Do you feel resentful that your child asks you to play the dolls first thing every day in the morning when your eyes aren't open yet?

Establish a rule that you get to sit and drink coffee for 10 minutes until you are available to play. Is your baby going to complain? Perhaps. But they're also going to begin to learn that you also have needs. If your own needs are met, you will be a healthier parent, and your child will see a great example of how in a relationship to advocate for their own needs.

- **Re-Think Your View about the Problem.**

Think of something that your child does that drives you insane or disturbs you. Does the high-pitch shriek of your toddler get under your skin? Does your food throwing baby make you want to scream? First, ask what your child gets out of this action that you ask "evil." Is it your focus? Or is it more of a reaction? For a child who tries to get some attention, a parent's negative response is good enough. Your angry reaction keeps the behavior going.

Think about why you are so disturbed by this action. In front of people, are you embarrassed? Did you decide that this is an "evil" activity because it is something that adults do not consider appropriate? Any of these habits can be irritating, but they are suitable for growth and do not harm your child or anyone else. The less you get panic about them, the better they will be done.

- **Keep Fewer Expectations.**

We forget, sometimes that our children are just children! It will only set them up for disappointment and give them reasons to disappoint you by making standards that are not age-appropriate for your children. Do you expect your child's table manners to be right, to sit down for long meals, or to welcome all your friends and family? Teaching and modeling these "adult" behaviors to your children will allow your kids to do them, but keep your standards in check, mostly if your child has not napped or is hungry.

Teaching and modeling "adult" behaviors to your children will allow your kids to do them, but keep your standards maintained. The vacation season is when these undesirable habits surface when children are distracted at various times by large events or eating and sleeping. Some children are more introverted or shy about talking to adults and feel awkward. There is less room for resentment if you lower your standards.

- **Remember that This Phase Will End.**

Do you recall the awful first weeks of a baby at home? You didn't sleep; you fed a tiny being every two hours. The stage felt like it would never end for most parents, but it will, and so will each step. If at 3 am your 12 hours of a whole night sleeper has just begun to wake up, or your veggie-loving kid can eat macaroni and cheese, note that most unwanted habits are stages of ends.

- **You can Share Emotional Responsibility.**

Are you asking your partner to change the diaper for your kid, drop your son off at soccer, or help you get on her shoes? Sure! Of course! But do you share as a parent your emotional responsibilities? For parents, asking for tangible or physical support is simpler. Share with your partner if you're concerned about how your child is in school or feel frustrated by all the emotions that come with being a mom. It's not appropriate for you to bear the world's weight on your shoulders.

- **Stay Connected.**

As children who feel linked listen more, feel less stressed, and prefer positive habits, communicating with your child will make your job as a parent easier. If your child demonstrates bad behavior, first attempt to communicate with your child before discussing the bad behavior. The conduct may manifest a need for affection, feelings of abandonment or loneliness, or other yuck feelings.

Connecting with your child daily, outside of the discipline, is also essential. Kids who feel related to their parents have greater self-esteem, are more comfortable, and make better choices.

- **Be a Coach of Your Kids.**

Becoming a child coach and not controlling your child by helicopter or authoritative parenting is the next aspect of improving negative conduct. Think of yourself as a life coach for your kids, someone who will inspire them to make healthy choices and model appropriate behaviors. How will they be ready to make decisions for themselves if you monitor your child?

- **See the Situation Through Your Kid's Eyes.**

Parents ignore the emotions of children several times because they see them as immature or overdramatic. Take a step back, don't judge, and see the situation from the eyes of your child when your child is upset. Doing so would make it easy to be empathetic and validate the emotions of your child. It will get you together and let your child know that telling you their sad feelings is healthy.

- **Be a Parent of Child You Have, Not You Wanted.**

You needed an athlete, and you got a brain, didn't you? Throw away all of your worries about what your child will be like before they were born and take a good look at the child you have right now. For parents of multiple children, this is particularly relevant. Every child differs from the others and should be parented to fit their needs, with different strengths, defects, and personalities. In parenting, there is no one size works all, and once you parent the child you have, your role as a parent will feel much more straightforward.

2.2 How to Strengthen Parent-Child Relationships?

It takes dedication and effort to improve parent-child ties. Parenting is a difficult job, but by maintaining a close relationship and open communication with your children, parents can remain connected to them throughout all life stages. Further, a strong parent-child connection makes parenting more comfortable, as children feeling more connected to their parents are more likely to listen, help, and follow directions. Children who think related are often more involved in communicating about friends or school issues with their parents. Here are some simple tips that families can use to deepen parents' and children's bonds.

- **Tell Your Kids that You Love Them.**

Tell children that every day, no matter their age, you love them. Parents should ensure that children know that even on trying days or after disagreements, even if you did not like their behavior, remember you love them. Conflict is the primary time for parents to show their love to their children. To strengthen relationships, a simple "I love you" does tons.

- **Play with Your Kids.**

The idea is to get down on the floor and play with your kids. You can play with dolls, balls, board games, or sing songs. No matter what you play, it's just enjoying each other and committing to paying your undivided attention. Let your children see your dumb side. Older children enjoy playing cards, chess, and computer games, while younger children enjoy playing any game with their parents.

- **You can Establish a Special Name.**

Make a personal name that is optimistic or a hidden code word for your child that you can use with each other. As a simple reinforcement of your love, use the name. Without causing undue embarrassment to the child, the code word can remove a child from an awkward situation.

- **Make Bedtime Rituals.**

Reading books for bedtime or telling children tales establishes lifelong rituals. Bedtime is a separate time from other activities and developing a ritual. It makes kids feel safer. Bedtime can also be the only time working parents share with their kids, so try and make it calm and enjoyable. As soon as kids start reading, make them read you a page, chapter, or short book. Even most teens also love the tradition of a parent, especially saying goodnight.

- **Teach Your Kids about Spirituality and Faith.**

Teach your baby about your religion and values. Tell her why and what you believe. Say your child's time to ask questions and honestly answer them. Strengthen such lessons regularly.

- **Involve Your Kid to Help You.**

Parents mistakenly miss out on closeness possibilities by not allowing their children to assist them with different activities and tasks. After going to the store, unloading food is an excellent example of something kids of most ages can and should help with. Children feel strong when they help. By giving opinions, children can also help. Asking a kid with your dress which shoes look better lets him know that you appreciate his opinion. When you ask, be prepared to embrace the child's option and live with it.

- **Maintain a One to One Time.**

To establish one-on-one time, some parents have special nights or "standing dates" with their children. It is essential to enjoy each child individually, whether it is a stroll around the neighborhood, a trip to a playground, or a movie night with your kids. While for parents with many children, this is more of a challenge, it is achievable.

- **Respect Choice of Your Kids.**

You may not like the mismatched shirt and shorts of your child or love the way your child has put pictures in his bedroom. It is necessary to honor those choices, however. At a young age, children reach out for independence, and by being supportive and even looking the other way on occasion, parents can help foster those decision-making skills. After all, if a kid goes to daycare with a striped green shirt and pink shorts, it's OK.

- **Make Your Kids Your Priority.**

Your children need to know that in your life, you believe they are a priority. Children can notice excessive stress and see when they feel that you are not paying attention to them. Sometimes, part of parenthood does not worry about the little things and enjoy the children. They grow up so quickly, and it's special every day. When you have it, take advantage of your precious time together!

2.3 How to Parent Different Personalities?

Your kids were born under the same roof, but they couldn't be more distinct from their personalities. How is that? Learn about these temperament features and how to adapt your style of parenting to your children's personalities. If you are a parent of more than one kid, you're probably shocked at how different your kids look. One could be quiet and easy-going, while the other could be very social and enthusiastic. One takes a shift in development, while another will require extra time to adjust. In the same parents' company, in the same home environment, and the same society, children were raised, but they approach life very differently. Ok, what gives? Sometimes, temperament is the key.

- **What is Temperament?**

Temperament applies to both our personality attributes and life reactions. When considering temperament, psychologists and researchers typically look at five elements. Such features include:

- Intensity emotional
- Level of Operation
- Tolerance for irritation
- Reaction to new individuals
- Reaction to alteration

Each individual is born with the characteristics and temperament of his or her unique personality. Temperament is not induced by something you have done or have not done, nor is it a cultural product, although a child's atmosphere can play a role in how he perceives himself and adapts to life. An understanding of temperament can assist parents in tailoring their approach to the needs of their children.

- **Know Each of Your Child.**

As for who they are, you must be obvious. Each child has interests, dislikes, and goals of their own. When they are hungry, sad, or need time alone, you can identify their moods. With each of them, you invest time. You can take your oldest for a grocery shopping experience with you. You may want to teach him about shopping and meal planning, and he was leaving for college. As you drive him to school, your middle son and you can chat. Your youngest, while holding your hand, wants to watch movies with you. This way, you will be these three parents at the same moment.

- **Build Understanding.**

Throughout the day, your child dawdles, lingering over every activity, while you enjoy crossing stuff off your to-do list. You enjoy meeting new people with your partner, but your child would prefer to stay at home. Frequently, there is a mismatch between the temperament of an infant and the temperament of a parent. This mismatch can contribute to conflict. It enables you to step back, gain insight, and stay patient by knowing your disposition and that of your child.

 It will help if you are looking for options and compromises instead of being upset. For example, by providing plenty of advance notice before a new event, giving information on what to expect and how to react, and engaging in small group activities instead of larger meetings where possible, you can support an introverted child. In this case, some parents think that a compromise works well, e.g., 'I know you don't love parties. Let's go for 45 minutes; then we're going to come home.

- **Do Not Compare Your Child with Each Other.**

You may have been compared to another member of the family as a young child. Consequently, you can see the unique value that the universe brings to each of your children. You must be aware not to say," Why can't you be more like your brother? Often, because they are obedient or have an easy-going personality, we have children who raise them look 'easy' when the other child is rebellious, stubborn, or moody. It's natural to want all of them to be alike, but it's not true.

- **Advocate Your Child.**

Our society continues to reward quiet, docile actions. You've probably faced criticism from well-meaning family or friends if you have a kid with high energy and strong emotions. Understanding that temperament attributes are unique and inherent will help remove the strain, helping you see your child's traits as possible strengths. You can better react in ways that are advantageous to your child to negative remarks, e.g.," Yeah, she is spirited and independent. She knows what she wants exactly. She works to learn to negotiate.

In the parenting toolbox, the theories about temperament are just one tool. Knowing personality traits will help you develop a deeper understanding of your child's needs and how best to support their development. However, it is noteworthy that temperament is just one part of a child's growth and experience. Behaviors may be caused by the climate, disease, cultural expectations, and disabilities in development.

Temperament is not always a definite trait. Kids with introverted characteristics of personality will learn to become more social. Self-regulation can be mastered by a child with a 'fast temper.' Use your temperament awareness as a guide, but avoid putting labels (e.g., shy, hot-headed, stubborn) on your child that could limit her growth.

- **Keep Your Needs Separate.**

The divergence of parental expectations and temperamental style from that of our children is another common parenting challenge. A parent may assume that a child "needs" a lot of social interaction, for instance, when the parent wants it. Being clear about your style and needs of parenting will help you maintain healthy boundaries and see your kids as people.

Chapter 3: Stress Management of Kids

3.1 Recognizing Stress in Your kids

In terms of looking after their children's mental health, parents play a crucial role, including keeping stress and anxiety to a safe minimum. But parents must first be able to identify the multiple signs of stress in children to comfort a child who is overcome by worries. The child is different, but when deciding whether their child is dealing with anxiety, parents may use common signs and behaviors as a litmus test.

- **Physical Symptoms of Stress.**

Stress can physically affect our bodies and health for both adults and children. It's incredibly essential to rule out any problems that may cause the matter when deciding if stress is the reason behind a physical symptom. Always seek advice from your child's pediatrician.

Widespread childhood physical symptoms of stress include:

- **Changes in Eating Habits.**

Stress will interfere with the eating habits of your infant. Some can appear to overeat, whereas there may be a lack of appetite for others. In children, stress can also cause tummy distress, and you can find symptoms of indigestion.

- Headache
- Problems with the sleep cycle, such as problems falling asleep, remaining asleep or recurrent nightmares
- Bedwetting activities

It is important to stress that, besides stress, these physical signs may point to other problems, making communicating with your child's pediatrician completely necessary to rule out other possibilities.

- **Emotional Symptoms of Stress.**

Stress has a significant influence on our emotional state and skills, and as a result, children will see a decline in school success, sports, and other aspects of their lives. It is not always easy to recognize behavioral and emotional signs of stress, so parents should keep a close eye on children shortly after their divorce and after any other significant changes in their child's life.

Popular childhood emotional and behavioral symptoms of stress include:

- Regressive conduct, or when a child participates in actions that are not acceptable for their age
- Thumb-sucking, throwing tantrums, engaging in baby-talk, or the inability to sleep without a night light can be examples of regressive behavior in older children.
- Fresh fears or recurring ones
- Inability to calm down or relax
- The trouble with their feelings being monitored

- **Crying**

Crying can be one of a stressed baby's first and most common reactions. It is a signal to the caregiver that, in normal circumstances, they do not feel well or need something. A child who faces stress will weep more than usual. If your child weeps uncontrollably, you're trying to figure out what's causing them stress.

- o **No Eye Contact**

When they are stressed, babies tend to avoid eye contact. They could be stressed if your baby's gaze was usual before, and now they stop looking into your eyes. Lack of eye contact may suggest autism spectrum disorders or visual impairment in certain instances.

When they are under chronic stress, babies can look inexpressive. You could feel the absence of emotions on your face. When they feel afraid and stressed, babies may refuse to eat. However, you can also check for any potential cause of sickness or constipation if your baby is not eating. Some babies may resist new foods in later childhood stages, especially when they transition from breastfeeding to eating solid foods, because they may still want to breastfeed.

When working with their children to alleviate stress and anxiety, co-parents may often want to employ a mental health practitioner's assistance. Much-needed insights into your children's mental health can be given by the child or adolescent therapists and give your family the resources you need to get back on the right track.

3.2 How the Parents Can Help Kids Relieve Stress?

Children might not have to think about jobs, expenses, or what to prepare for dinner, but that doesn't mean that they're not facing stress every day. Before a class lecture, maybe your son gets butterflies, or maybe your daughter feels a little sick before any soccer game.

Every child varies, and so are their stress causes and responses. It could make them sweat or fidget or trigger them to pound their hearts. They can become overwhelmed or even feel dizzy or nauseous. Knowing some active ways to cope with daily stress is suitable for children and their parents, too.

- **Encourage Your Kids to Face the Fears.**

We stop them because we are frightened of circumstances. The fear, however, is preserved by the avoidance of anxiety-provoking circumstances. If a child confronts his or her worries, the child will realize that, over time, the anxiety gradually declines on its own. For a long time, the body does not stay nervous because there is a body mechanism that calms the body down. Usually, if you remain in an anxiety-provoking situation, the anxiety will decrease within 20-45 minutes.

- **Tell Your Child That Being Imperfect is Okay.**

We should recognize that it is essential for our kids to excel in sports, education, and success circumstances. But sometimes we forget that there is a need for children to be children. If 85 percent is good, but not good enough, school is motivated by ratings, not by the enjoyment of learning. It is not to suggest that it is not necessary to aspire. It is essential to encourage your child to work hard, but acknowledging and embracing your child's errors and imperfections are equally important.

- **Pay Attention to Positives.**

Anxious and depressed kids can get lost in negative thinking and self-criticism several times. They will concentrate on how half-empty the glass is instead of half full and think about future events. The more you can reflect on your child's positive qualities and the beneficial aspects of a situation, the more it can remind your child to reflect on the positive ones.

- **Organize Relaxing Activities.**

To relax and be children, kids need time. Sadly, often even enjoyable events, such as sports, can become more about achievement than pleasant. Instead, it is essential to make sure that your child plays solely for the sake of fun. It could include a daily routine for your child to play with toys, play a game, play a sport (without being competitive), do yoga, paint, have a tea party, play a game, or be dumb.

- **Model Positive Thinking, Self-Care, and Approach Behavior.**

Your kid is going to do what you do. So if you avoid circumstances that provoke anxiety, your child will, too. If you face your problems, your child will, too. Your child will understand that self-care is a significant part of life if you take care of yourself and plan time for your own needs. If you look for the positive in the circumstances, your child will, too. Kids learn attitudes by watching their parents. So when you think of the psychological well-being of your child, think of your own as well.

- **Help Your Child to Share the Stress Factor with You.**

When your child tells you that he or she is afraid or worried, don't say, "No, you're not!" or "You're all right." That's not supporting your child. It will make your child feel that you are not listening or not understanding him or her. Instead, affirm the experience of your child by saying things such as, "Yeah, you sound afraid. What are you concerned about?" And have a conversation about the feelings and concerns of your child.

- **Help Your Child to Solve the Problem.**

Help your child solve issues after you have validated your child's feelings and have proven that you appreciate your child's perspective and listen to what your child has to say. For your kid, this does not mean solving the issue. It means helping to find potential options for your kids. That is nice if your child can create solutions. If not, build some possible options for your child and ask your child to select the solution they feel will work best.

- **Stay Calm.**

To decide how to respond in the circumstances, children look to their parents. We all saw a trip and fall for a young child and then look to their parents to see how to respond. The infant cries if the parent is concerned. It is because the child is searching for a cue to their parents how to react to the situation.

Kids of all ages pick up on the thoughts of their parents and resonate with them. Your child will be stressed if you are nervous and feel a rise in his or her anxiety. And you have to control your pressure because you want to reduce your child's anxiety. It can mean slowing your speech purposefully, having a few deep breaths to relax, and ensuring that your facial expression represents that you are relaxed.

- **Practice Relaxation Exercises.**

To support your child to relieve their stress and anxiety, sometimes straightforward calming exercises are essential. It may mean asking your child to take a few long, deep breaths (and taking your child with you for a few long breaths so that your child can match your pace). Or it can mean asking your child to imagine him or herself relaxing somewhere, such as the seaside or relaxing in a hammock in the backyard. Tell your child to close their eyes and visualize the image-related sounds, smells, and sensations. Close your eyes, for instance, and imagine yourself on a beach. When the waves come, go away, listen to the sound of surfing out and in. Listen to the sound of seagulls in the distance, taking off. Now, concentrate on the sensation under your fingertips of the warm sand and the sun warming your skin. During stress-provoking periods, your kid can do these strategies on his or her own.

- **Never Give Up.**

A persistent struggle maybe stress and anxiety. Sometimes, over time, the root of a child's anxiety shifts so that it can feel as if you're continually putting out fires. Your child will acquire knowledge for how to lower his / her anxiety level and deal with anxiety-provoking circumstances with the repetition of anxiety and stress management strategies. Repetition is the answer, so keep it up!

3.3 Shaping Great Kids

A perfect way to educate children about new habits is the process of "shaping." Shaping is a psychology-based, step-by-step method. It includes teaching a child one small move at a time with a new ability. Before a new step is conducted, each step is reinforced. Then, kids can master more complex duties.

- **Examples of Shaping.**

If he has never cleaned his room before, asking your preschooler to clean his room is not likely to be effective. Thus, shaping will entail teaching him one step at a time rather than expecting him to set his bed, put his toys away, and clean the room.

You could start by teaching him to pull up his bed blankets. Then, for a few days, after he does that regularly, you could focus on making his bed neater. Then it would help if you worked on making his bed and cleaning up his toys for a few days.

When he shows you that he can regularly manage specific steps, you can move on to other things, such as vacuuming his room. Eventually, on his own, he'll be able to clean his entire room.

- **Appreciate Your Kids at Each Step.**

Praise is a wonderful way of influencing the conduct of a child. If you want your child to do chores regularly, for instance, compliment him when you catch him tossing something in the garbage can or placing a dish in the sink.

Make your appreciation concrete so that he understands why you appreciate him. "Rather than saying," Good job, "say," Great job of putting the dish in the sink as soon as you finished with it. When you put things away, I like it. It helps him realize the value of acting responsibly.

- **Use Attention and Ignoring.**

Since it is safe to do so, give your child the most attention while doing well, and overlook any minor misbehavior. If you want to influence your child's actions when treating others with respect, when he uses his manners, give him a lot of positive attention. Ignore him, then, when he is somewhat rude. When he says, "Get me a beer," pretend you're not going to hear him. But give him your full attention as soon as he asks politely, "May I have a beer, please." It shows him that the only way to get what he wants is by using etiquette.

- **Provide Plenty of Pre-Teaching.**

Pre-teaching clarifies your child about what conduct is expected about him. Before you enter a scenario, teach him the rules. "Remind him, for instance," At Grandma's place, we have to take off our shoes before we go inside. And inside her home, we only use walking feet. A daily reminding of the laws, with reminders about the consequences of violating the rules, offers children a chance to obey.

- **Guide Your Child What to Do.**

You need to teach positive behavior if you want your kid's behavior to improve. Teach him what he should do when he feels upset, instead of screaming, "Don't hit your brother." It could be great alternate skills to teach him to use his vocabulary or tell an adult when he is angry.

- **Provide Logical Reasoning.**

Logical effects are directly linked to the wrongdoing and can be a perfect tool for behavioral shaping. Take away the right to play with the toys your kid does not pick up if you want your child to begin cleaning up after himself. It quickly tells him that he has to start cleaning up after himself if he wants to continue playing with his toys.

- **Develop a Reward System.**

A reward system is a perfect way to influence your behavior if you are working on a new behavior. Don't just expect perfection. Reward some close approximations, instead. For instance, when you want your child to be more obedient, please don't suggest that he must comply with anything for a full week before he gets a reward. Instead, consider a scheme of the token economy where he will receive tokens each time he is compliant. Initially, reward him if he rolls his eyes or protests but still does as you ask. It makes it tough to obtain the incentive over time. But initially, reward the behavior you want to see with incremental steps.

3.4 Protecting Kids from Molesters

As all we cannot always be with our kids right there, we need to know that they are still trustworthy adults in controlled circumstances.

- **Notice Who is in Your Kid's Life?**

Check whether your child's daycare, kindergarten, and after-school services have an open-door policy, along with either a real open door or a window into any space where children spend time. (Many classrooms have a small window built into each door at least.) Ideally, this should be paired with supervisors' daily, unexpected visits. In reality, there should be a door with a window for any situation that's innately private (such as counseling), so you still can observe.

Do not avoid checking her history and references if you are using a nanny or another unsupervised caregiver. Fall in unannounced on occasion. And make it clear that without your permission, you don't want your child left in anyone else's care because it's likely that a caregiver's friend or family member may have sexual conduct issues, says Johnson. It is especially important if treatment occurs in a home where there might be other grown-ups or older children around.

Please get to know the coaches, pastors, teachers, and other adults in your child's world and see how they communicate with her. Show up to practice, get interested in events, and volunteer in the classroom. And if something sounds wrong, chat and compare notes to other parents. Listen up when your kids share concerns or awkward feelings and strategize as a group on how you can ensure each other's children's safety.

It's also necessary to get to know your children's friends. Pay particular attention to friendships involving older children, which can lead to circumstances of insecurity. More than a third of people who assault kids sexually are themselves under the age of 18. A child cannot realize that his acts against another child are harmful in many cases.

You may need to concentrate on particular concerns based on your child's developmental stage and discuss (or avoid) those subjects.

- **Use Accurate Language.**

Skip the code words, and tell them exactly what points of the body can be touched badly. It eliminates possible misunderstandings and increases the willingness of your child to speak about sexual circumstances.

- **Tell Your Kids What is Private.**

Tell her that no one can touch her private parts except herself, her parents, and her doctor (and caregiver if your child's still in diapers). She will tell you if someone does, and you won't be angry.

- **Tell Him to be the Owner of His Body.**

Has a stranger ever stirred the hair of your boy, telling you how beautiful he is? Your inclination may be to accept the conduct respectfully. Yet it is a perfect moment for teaching. Saying, "I don't feel comfortable with someone we don't know touching models of my children" to your child that it's all right to say "no" to touch, even from "good" people outside.

- **Be a Protective Shield for Your Children.**

You may assume this is obvious to your kid, but clearly state that if she ever feels confused or frightened about something, she can tell you and that you will support and love her no matter what has happened.

- **Reinforce Boundaries.**

Help your child if he tries to say "No, thank you" to relatives' embraces or kisses. If your son squirts away as Grandma bends to kiss him, you might tell, "Right now, Vincent isn't really in a kissing mood, and that's all right, isn't it, Grandma?"

- **Make Them Comfortable to Share Feelings with You Anytime.**

Do not wait until you suspect that there's something wrong. "Children need to hear that if anyone acts sexually with them and that they should still come to you, it's never their fault. By doing it, you help take away the most effective weapons of the perpetrator-shame and fear. Logan ("I realize to realize that people cannot touch your private parts or ask you to touch theirs") says that Bath time is an opportunity to learn about bodies and boundaries. "Or use current events:" There are adults who want to do inappropriate stuff with kids, and it depends on you as a parent to keep your kid safe. If you feel awkward, you can always come to me.

These were the Tips you can tell to your kids below age 9; now, I will share more points to say to your kids above nine.

Continue the debate. The peers could sexually threaten them as kids close to puberty. Indeed, the own developing sexuality of your child can get him into circumstances that can be readily taken advantage of by abusers. Look for reasons to talk about this; it may provide ways for your child to escape or get out of awkward situations with peers by brainstorming. Emphasize that when someone mistreats her, it's never a child's fault.

- **Monitor Devices.**

Via smartphones and gaming systems that can be linked to the Internet, children can quickly, and sometimes unintentionally, access porn. "In our practice, we see a record-high number of these cases," says Dr. Julie Medlin. "Many parents do not know that their children can access porn in this way so easily, nor do they know how much of a negative effect such exposure can have on the sexuality of the child." Consult the user guide of your computer to allow parental controls, restrict access to certain adult content games, and monitor web surfing, chat functions, and purchases.

- **Help Your Kids to Identify Trusted Adults.**

Many children cannot get themselves directly to parents to report sexual assault, Sax says. So she wants children to be taught to seek out adults that they feel safe turning to when they are troubled by something. She adds that before anyone acts on the issue, they can continue to tell you. Teachers and school counselors must report alleged violence to authorities by statute, and all adults who suspect violence are required to report.

Chapter 4: Raising Confidence in Your Child

Although it may often be typical for an adolescent to lack confidence, individuals with self-esteem problems typically see themselves differently than how others see them. When they do things like beginning high school or college and developing new friendships and relationships, low self-esteem can be incredibly difficult for young kids. Please keep reading to understand the self-esteem issues that your teen can create and some methods to help your child feel great about themselves and their abilities.

4.1 Self-Esteem for Kids

For kids, positive self-esteem is essential as it encourages them to try new things, take healthy chances, and solve problems. Their learning and growth, in turn, will be productive and will set them up for a bright and stable future. A high self-esteem young person is more likely to exhibit positive behavioral traits, such as:

- Independent and mature acting
- Taking pride in their achievements/accomplishments
- Accepting and coping responsibly with anger
- Checking new stuff and problems
- Assisting others wherever possible

- **How Can Low Self-Esteem Affect Your Kids?**

They prefer to avoid circumstances where they think there's a chance of failure, humiliation, or making errors when someone has low self-esteem. These may include working in a school, making friends, and pursuing new things, all of which are essential components of a healthy teenage life.

If there is no consideration and treatment of low self-esteem, it can lead to problems such as:

- The trouble with relationships or difficulty making friends
- Negative moods such as feeling sad, nervous, humiliated, or irritated
- Low-motivated
- A bad description of the body
- Previous Sexual Behavior
- Drinking alcohol and taking medicine to make you feel better

- **Causes of Low Self-Esteem in Kids**

As a result of your kids' experiences, and how they cope with circumstances, how they feel about themselves can result in low self-esteem.

In adolescents, the most common causes of low self-esteem are:

- Parents, care takers, or those who play an essential role in their lives are not helpful.
- Companions that are poor influences
- Stressful incidents in life, including divorce or moving houses
- Violence or trauma
- Bad results or ambitious expectations at school
- Mood disturbances, such as anxiety
- Anxiety and depression
- Intimidation or isolation
- Continuous medical conditions

- **Signs of Low Self-Esteem:**

More than likely, a child with low self-esteem would have negative thoughts about their worth and importance as an individual.

Some specific signs that low self-esteem is present in your child include:

- Avoiding new stuff and not taking up possibilities
- An unloved and unwanted feeling
- To accuse others of their own mistakes
- -not being able to cope with usual anger levels
- -negative self-talk and comparisons with others
- Anxiety over failure or humiliation
- Had trouble making friends
- Low motivation and interest levels
- Such kid does not take compliments and exhibits mixed feelings of tension or stress.

You can do things to help your child have good self-esteem, but it is also important to note that overtime evolves and changes very often in adolescent self-esteem. If your child does not instantly exhibit signs of positive self-esteem, it does not necessarily mean that you are doing anything wrong!

4.2 How can Parents Affect Children Self-esteem?

The responsiveness of parents to their babies very early in life influences the growth of self-confidence and self-esteem. Summoning an image of a doting parent reacting to a baby with loving sounds, engaged chatter, concentrated attention, and cuddling takes little effort. The kid smiles, and the parent smiles back. Parents continue to react and mimic what the baby is doing as the child matures. Parental mirroring expresses approval, appreciation, and respect through early childhood, puberty, and young adulthood. It significantly leads to the growth of self-esteem and self-confidence.

Children usually receive scant mirroring or encouragement when parental participation is minimal. They have no one who reflects them that they are attractive, admirable, or worthwhile. When parents are over-involved, there are few possibilities for the child to self-reflect and have their positive thoughts and feelings through their undue influence over how their children perceive themselves in the world. The growth of self-confidence and self-esteem are impaired in both instances.

The most significant parenting flaws that crush the confidence of children:

- **Letting Kids Escape from the Responsibilities.**

Although you might think that duties will weigh down your children and contribute to their stress level, participating in around the house will help them become more responsible citizens.

Performing age-appropriate duties allows them to feel a satisfaction of mastery and achievement. Therefore, when you tell your child to help with the laundry or carry out the garbage, duties are opportunities for children to see themselves as qualified and capable.

- **Stopping Them from Making Mistakes.**

It is hard to watch your kid lose, get dismissed, or screw up with something. So many parents run in when this happens to save children before they fall. But stopping them from making mistakes robs them of the chance to learn how to rebound.

Mistakes can be the most outstanding teacher in life, whether your child forgets their cleats before a significant soccer game or gets a few questions wrong on their math quiz. Each one is a chance for them to develop the mental strength the next time they need to do better.

- **Preventing Them from Their Emotions**

It's tempting to cheer up your kids when they're sad, or if they're upset, calm them down. But how we react to our children's emotions has a significant effect on the growth of their emotional intelligence and self-esteem.

Help your children recognize and teach them how to self-regulate what activates their emotions. Please provide them with a mechanism that helps to clarify how they feel so that in the future, they can have a simpler time coping with those feelings in a socially acceptable way.

- **Accepting a Victim Mentality**

Using words like "we cannot buy new shoes like the other children because we come from a bad situation" reinforces that much of life's circumstances are out of their control for your child.

You can encourage them to take constructive steps instead of encouraging your children to hold pity parties or exaggerate their misfortunes (e.g., setting up a lemonade stand to have savings to buy things they want or need).

Children who appreciate their life options are more secure in their ability to build for themselves a better future.

- **Becoming Overprotective**

Sure, you are saving a lot of worry by holding your child within a safe bubble. But keeping them insulated from difficulties slows their progress. See yourself not as a defender, but as a guide. And when it is scary to let go, encourage your children to experience life. You will give them the chance to build confidence in their ability to cope with whatever life throws their way.

- **Seeking Perfection:**

High expectations are reasonable, but there are risks of expecting too much. When children see expectations as too high, they may not even bother trying or feel as though they are never going to measure up.

Instead, give consistent long-term goals and set goals along the way. For instance, going to college is a long-term expectation, helping them build short-term goals (e.g., having good grades, completing their homework, reading) along the way.

4.3 Self-Esteem Building Activities for Kids

Here are some games and operational activities that can develop the self-confidence of a child.

- **"I am" Activity**

Is your child proud, or do they seem to be overly self-critical of their achievements? With this Activity, you will address the possibility.

  - **What Do You Need for This Activity?**

Diagram or drawing paper, cutouts of magazine adjectives, glue, color pen or sketch pen

- **How to Perform?**

1. Say your child to write on a piece of paper the words that define them. It can be positive or negative.
2. Then ask them to reflect and make a list of just the positive things that people have said about them.
3. Paste the child's picture in the middle of the paper of the drawing or map.
4. Ask the child to use positive words, adjectives to relate, and fill in the picture area.
5. To reinforce positive beliefs about yourself, place the drawing sheet of paper in her room.

- **Listing Wins of Life**

Reminding them of their achievements is a successful way to improve the child's self-esteem.

- **What Do You Need for This Activity?**

A paper board, a pen

- **How to Perform?**

1. Give a pen and paper or notebook to your kid.
2. Start by writing down the list of achievements in life on the front page, leaving room at the bottom to add more later.
3. You may also ask her to list her wins every day, before she goes to bed, to remind the child of her potential.
4. Emphasize that not only are failures okay, but they are essential. Take time to consider when your child is working through a challenging moment successfully.

- **I am frightened, But ...**

For infants, fear is a normal feeling. Here's an exercise for kids to face and communicate about their fears.

- ○ **What Do You Need for This Activity?**

Pen and Paper

- ○ **How to Perform?**

1. Tell your child to list the things she's scared of doing. She may be terrified of going to swimming lessons, for example. Or she is afraid of making a class presentation.

The phrases need to be something like this:

I am fearful of signing up for the swim team because

I am scared to talk to you about this and that because

2. The second step is to imagine doing something that they are afraid of. Imagine registering or talking to that person for that swim team.
3. Ask them to write the potential consequences if they tried it every time the child notices down what they are afraid of. And get them to write something about possible positive results next to the bad outcome.

- • **Mother-Daughter Self-Esteem Activity**

Mother-daughter relationships tend to be healthy and yet riddled with fraught moments. For working on the girl's self-esteem, this practice taps into the mother-daughter bond.

- ○ **What Do You Need for This Activity?**

Poster or map sheets, drawing pens or ink pens

- ○ **How to Perform?**

1. With the word 'ME' stenciled on them, make two posters so that you can fill the letters with text.
2. Build another poster stenciled on them with the words "MY MOM" and another with "MY GIRL."
3. Give the child a poster of "ME" and "MY MOM" and ask her to fill it with good stuff about herself and her mother. Let the mom focus on the two remaining ones.
4. Let the posters be shared or the compliments they have for each other read.

- • **Assigning Chores with a Purpose**

The self-esteem of a child will get a fast boost when they know others trust them. What can be a better way to demonstrate that you trust your child than by giving them responsibility for a mission.

- ○ **How to Perform?**

1. Make a list of chores your child will do to care for the surrounding environment and animals.

For Example

Walking the dog, watering the gardens, or mopping the floor.

2. Any time the child completes the assignment, praise them but do not overdo it.
3. If they make errors, assist them in correcting the mistake, but do not concentrate on it. Chores will lead to building self-confidence in your child.

4.4 Tips to Improve Confidence in Kids

Since they are scared of failing or upsetting others, a child who lacks faith would be hesitant to attempt new or complicated stuff. Later in life, it will ultimately hold them back and discourage them from getting a good career. "Discouragement and fear are the enemies of the faith," he says. So, as a parent, as they try to tackle challenging tasks, it's your job to motivate and support your child.

- **Appreciate the Effort of Your Kids, No Matter They Win or Lose.**

The path is more important than the destination when you're growing up. So if your child completes his team's winning goal or unintentionally kicks it out of bounds, praise their effort, Pickhardt says. They should never feel shameful for trying. "Consistently trying hard builds more confidence over the long haul than doing well intermittently," he says.

- **Encourage Practice of Your Kids to Develop Competence.**

Motivate your child to learn whatever they are interested in, but do so without placing too much pressure on them. A piano prodigy, Harmony Shu, told Ellen DeGeneres that when she was just three years old, she began practicing. In the confident belief that enhancement will follow, practice invests effort.

- **Let Your Kids Figure Out the Problems by Themselves.**

If you do your child's hard work, they will never gain the skill or trust to sort out issues independently. Parental support should resist self-help trust and find out on the child's own. In other words, better than straight A's, the child gets a few B's and C's, as long as they recognize how to fix the issues and do the job.

- **Let Kids Act According to Their Age.**

Do not presume that your child would behave like a grown-up. If a child thinks that it is good enough only to perform as well as parents, that unrealistic expectation can discourage effort, "he says." "Striving to meet standards of advanced age will decrease confidence."

- **Appreciate Curiosity.**

The endless stream of questions from a child can sometimes be tiresome, but it should be encouraged. When children start school, those from households who have inspired curious questions have some advantage over their classmates as they have had practice taking information from their parents. They know how to learn better and quicker, in other words.

- **Present Your Child with New Challenges.**

Show your child that they can pursue and attain small goals to achieve a significant achievement, such as riding a bike without training wheels. By increasing obligations that must be fulfilled, parents will foster faith.

- **Avoid Making Short-Cuts.**

A lack of confidence may be conveyed through preferential care. Privilege is no substitute for a trust.

- **Never Criticize Your Child Performance.**

More than condemning his or her efforts, nothing will deter your child. It's good to provide useful feedback and make suggestions, but never tell them that they are doing a poor job. If your child is afraid of failure because they fear that you're going to be frustrated or disappointed, they're never going to try new stuff.

- **Consider Mistakes as Building Blocks of Confidence.**

It builds trust when you learn from errors. But this only happens when you, as a parent, see mistakes as an opportunity to learn and develop. Do not be over-protective of your kids. Encourage them now and then to screw up and understand how they will handle the job better next time.

- **Show Them New Doors to Experiences.**

"As a parent, they are responsible for" increasing the exposure to life and interactions so that the child can create trust in dealing with a larger world. Exposing kids to new experiences shows them that they can overcome it, no matter how frightening and different something is.

- **Do not Tell Your Kids When You Are Worried about Them.**

The child may also perceive parental concern as a vote of no trust." Expressing parental confidence engenders the faith of the child.

- **Praise Your Kids When They Deal with Adversity.**

Life is not balanced. It is not easy, and at some level, every child will have to learn that. Parents should point out how enduring these struggles can improve their strength when they face hardships. Reminding your child that every path to success is filled with setbacks is crucial.

- **Provide Your Support but Not Too Much.**

Giving too much support too early will reduce the ability of the child to self-help. Making parental assistance dependent on the self-help of the child first can build trust. Making parental aid dependent on the self-help of the child first can build trust.

- **Appreciate Kids to Try Innovative Things.**

Parents should reward their children for doing new stuff, whether it is going out for the traveling basketball team or riding on their first roller coaster. You can try this; you are brave! Comfort comes from sticking to the familiar; to dare the new and different, courage is required.

- **Celebrate the Excitement of Learning.**

The route is more valuable than the destination when you're growing up. So if your child completes his team's winning goal or unintentionally kicks it out of bounds, praise their effort. They should never feel shameful for trying. Consistently trying hard builds more confidence over the long haul than doing well intermittently.

- **Do not Allow Your Kids to Escape Reality by Wasting Their Time on the Internet.**

Do not encourage your child to hide behind the screen of a computer. Alternatively, allow them to participate in the natural world of real people. Confidence in the virtual environment (although significant) is not the same as the trust in the real world that physical efficiency brings.

Be authoritative but not forceful. The confidence of the child to self-direct may be diminished if parents are too strict or demanding.

Chapter 5: Positive Parenting Tips

To different people, positive parenting means slightly different. But the central concept could be summarized in this way:

By rewarding and promoting their better instincts, positive parenting stresses warm, positive family experiences, and guides kids. Positive parenting aims to interact with children, give them comfort and support. It builds circumstances that make it easier for children to act cooperatively and constructively.

5.1 Positive Parenting Tips for Kids of Age 0-1 Year

To become safe and happy, babies need positive care and guidance. You may have several concerns about instruction and discipline in your baby's first year. For healthy growth, the first years of your child's life are crucial. In the early years, you may face hundreds of parenting decisions about sleeping, nourishing, and taking care of your infant. In these first years, your child's interactions will undoubtedly play a role in influencing the adult they will become.

- **Social and Emotional Baby Development**

Although your baby cannot speak to express feelings and needs yet, your baby always interacts with you. A way of communicating needs is with smiles, eye contact, and how your baby adheres to your arms. These are early social and psychological abilities that are still in development. These abilities will mature as your baby grows and will help your child understand and navigate her world.

Your baby's first year of growth is fantastic. Your baby will learn how to travel, how to locate and use parts of her body. To understand your emotional responses, facial expressions, and how to use words, your baby will be watching you.

- **Stimulating Baby**

All your baby activates the brain hears, sees, senses, touches, feels, and tastes in these early months. Security, protection, and well-being are strengthened by positive consideration, playful interactions, calm responses from you all.

Simple baby toys can help your baby build skills in practice. Playful, open-ended, and low vital experiences are far more critical than formal, linear instruction, though the practice is essential. Sing songs, read stories, speak openly, and share your baby's experiences. Make eye contact and, with gentle, kind hands, touch your infant. This kind of stimulation is even more necessary and helps grow the brain of your infant. While it can be enjoyable for toys with music and chat, these are not replacements for meaningful, interactive interactions with you.

- **Safety of Your Baby**

It is time to make sure that your home is a healthy place when a baby becomes part of your family. Keep notice of things around the house for items that could be unsafe for your kids. As a parent, ensuring that you build a healthy home for your baby is your responsibility. It will be great that you take the appropriate measures to ensure that your new baby is mentally and emotionally ready for you. To keep your baby healthy, here are a few tips:

Do not ever shake your kid! Babies have very weak muscles in the neck that cannot hold their heads yet. You can put damage to his brain or even cause his death if you shake your kid.

These are some points that you can do as a parent to help your kid.

- Speak to your toddler. She is finding your voice relaxing.

- Answer to the repeating sounds and adding words when your baby makes sounds. It will assist him with learning to use words.

- Please read it to your kids. It will help her develop words and sounds and understand them.
- Sing and play music with your son. It will help your baby grow a passion for music and support the growth of his brain.

- Praise your child and give her plenty of loving attention.

- Spend time cuddling your baby and holding it. It is going to make him feel cared for and protected.

- When she's alert and happy, play with your daughter. To take a break from playing, watch your baby closely for signs of being exhausted or fussy.

- When he begins to run and touch objects, he should not touch, distract your baby with toys and run him to safe places.

- To stop sudden infant death syndrome (commonly known as SIDS), ensure that you always put your baby to sleep on her back.

- Cover your baby from secondhand smoke and your family. Do not encourage anyone in your home to smoke.

- Place your baby in the back seat in a rear-facing car seat when riding in a car.

- Prevent your baby from choking by cutting into tiny bites of her food. Often, don't let her play with little toys and other stuff that might be easy to swallow for her.

- Don't let your child have something to play with that could cover her ears.

- Never bring hot liquids or food close to or while carrying your infant.

- For protecting the health of your child, vaccines (shots) are necessary. Your child must get the right shots at the right time because children can get serious diseases. Chat with your child's doctor to make sure your child's vaccines are up-to-date.

Physically and emotionally take care of yourself. Hard work can be parenting! Enjoying your new baby and becoming a supportive, caring parent is easier when you feel good about yourself.

For the first six months of a kid, breast milk serves all the needs of your infant. Your baby will experience new tastes and textures with safe, solid food between the ages of 6 and 12 months, but breast milk should still be a vital source of nutrition. Slowly and gently feed your child, encourage your child to try new tastes without pressure, and observe if he is still hungry.

5.2 Parenting Tips for Parents of Toddler from Age Group 1-2 Years

You know how it seems like to be in a state of continuous motion and emotion as a toddler's parent. Their everyday needs and activities will change right along with them as your child continues to grow and develop. You can closely observe what to expect regarding diet and nutrition, sleep, safety, health issues, and more during the toddler years.

- **Everyday Life**

Toddlers are fond of showing off their new physical abilities. For hours on end, they explore, climb, and play. Most of them enjoy doing simple things, such as finding rocks, pouring water in and out of big buckets, and playing simple games such as peek-a-boo.

The day of a younger child will rotate between feeding, sleeping, playing, and having changes in the diaper. An older toddler will have more opportunities to play and will be willing to participate in any activities that you do.

Toddlers going to daycare are also likely to enjoy watching the other children play. While they're too young to play together, your little one may enjoy playing with their toys while sitting near the other kids.

- **Nutrition of Your Toddler:**

The number of calories a child needs each day will vary depending on the child, any medical needs, and, of course, physical activity. Your toddler would need between 900 and 1,200 calories a day; the American Heart Association predicts. Most 1-year-olds need about 1,000 calories a day, and those calories can be divided into the day with three solid foods and two snacks.

Remember, practicing strange feeding habits is common for toddlers. At breakfast, they can eat many calories, graze the rest of the day, and then not starving at dinner. They may do the total opposite the next day. It can be challenging for toddler's moms, but for toddlers to do "cluster," feeding or have days where they eat more is considered a natural trend.

In general, children without food allergies should eat 2 ounces of meat or legumes, 3 ounces of corn, two portions of dairy products, 1 cup of vegetables, 1 cup of fruit, and three tablespoons of fat or oil each day. Although your toddler may refuse to eat dinner, they probably still get plenty of calories. The American Academy of Pediatrics says, in reality, that a reasonable rule for child portion sizes is that they should be around a quarter of the size of an adult portion.

However, the quality of food that your little one is consuming is more critical than counting calories for your toddler. Make sure your toddler consumes a healthy, large variety of nutritious foods. That's nothing if a toddler wants some ranch sauce to put on some carrots or likes to eat an oatmeal bowl for breakfast if it's sprinkled with brown sugar.

In general, these helpful tips on toddler feeding are offered by the American Academy of Pediatrics:

Give water or milk for toddler drinks only. The juice is also high in sugar and calories.

- **Snacks.**

Give your toddler two or three nutritious snacks a day.

- **Continuity is Essential.**

Do not make a big deal about food. If your toddler does not like to try a new meal, say " Yes, "remove the feed, and then give it another time again. The trick is not to make food a fight for control or apply negative emotions to it. Do not punish your child for not trying a new meal, but continue to deliver healthy snacks at frequent intervals.

Often it is common for toddlers to be fussy eaters. Enable some autonomy during mealtimes, and you may decrease food refusals. By age one and not longer than 18 months, most babies give up the bottle entirely. By 18 months, most children will move from a bouncy chair to a booster seat. Sitting in a booster seat often decreases mealtime tantrums, as your toddler can enjoy eating at the dining table with the rest of the family.

Children can get at least 30 minutes of organized physical activity each day, as well as one more hour or more of unstructured physical activity, according to the Society of Health and Physical Educators. These activities do not have to be a complicated-spending time in the park, or only taking your kid out for a walk around the neighborhood are good choices.

For toddlers, having enough physical activity is typically not problematic. Playing, for them, is work. The simple play helps toddlers improve motor skills further, learn essential concepts such as colors and numbers, and sharpen skills such as problem-solving, critical thinking, imagination, and more.

A busy toddler is always on the move, and it can be hard to keep them engaged and focused. As your toddler's attention span grows, and their conduct becomes more routine and manageable, you can find plenty of possibilities to try new things.

Different activities, both individual and group, are also a great way to help your child develop new talents, add structure to your child's day, encourage gross and fine motor skills, and encourage cognitive growth. Toddlers are instinctively curious, making this stage a great time for some groups of parents and children. There are several organized games for older toddlers, from soccer to yoga and music to movement.

You know how it seems like to be in a state of continuous motion and emotion as a toddler's parent. Their everyday needs and activities will change right along with them as your child continues to grow and develop. You can closely observe what to expect regarding diet and nutrition, sleep, safety, health issues, and more during the toddler years.

- **Health and Safety**

Whenever they are up, your toddler would undoubtedly want to be by your side most of the time. It is essential to some of the things that you do.

It is always more straightforward and faster for parents to do everything themselves. Still, it can keep them involved and teach valuable skills by encouraging your toddler to contribute in the smallest ways. Tell them to throw a napkin for you in the trash or encourage them to sweep alongside you using their toy broom.

Much of the toddlers' tasks are to clean up toys, put dirty laundry in a hamper, or put books back on the shelf. Your little one will be involved in helping you do chores as well. Enable an older child to help you wipe out messes, care for pets, and make your bed.

Talking to your child is essential to helping them learn improved language skills. In your talk, use descriptive terms that explain the color or size of items. You might also narrate what they do by saying stuff like, "You build with blocks." You've kicked over the blocks.

The best way to stay with your child is to get down on the floor in a child-friendly space alongside them but follow their lead. Play with your kids when they are playing with a doll. Just don't overthink about whether they're doing stuff "the right way." It is OK for bathtubs to be on the roof of the house in a child's imaginative play, and it's perfect for cars to speak.

- **Visiting the Doctor.**

Well-child visits for toddlers typically occur at 12, 15, 18, and 24 months of age with a pediatrician.

Screen Pediatricians for:

- At 18 months and two years, autism
- Problems of growth at 9, 18, and 24 months
- Obesity with a yearly body mass index beginning at the age of 24 months
- Risk assessment of lead screening at 6, 9, 12, 18, and 24 months
- Tuberculosis monitoring by one month, at six months, and then annually starting at 12 months to identify high-risk variables.
- In toddlers, common health problems include ear infections, colds,

and skin problems.

Speak to the pediatrician if you have questions about your child's development or concerns about sleeping or eating patterns, or behavior problems. Ask questions about the types of food you should present to your child and how to do so.

In your life, be sure to note any changes. Your child's well-being might be affected by a new relationship, a transfer to a new location, or a change in daycare.

It's also essential to ask your pediatrician about the potty-training readiness of your infant. Your pediatrician will help you recognize the right time to begin your child's training.

For toddlers, potty training is a significant achievement, and while it's a struggle for parents, most moms and dads look forward to post-diaper existence. But moving a child too fast on a potty train can end badly. Many potty training strategies promise success, but these approaches don't work once your child is ready. Before you tackle potty training, there are clear developmental milestones your child should achieve, and you must also consider either or not your toddler is genuinely interested in the potty, to start with.

- **Sleep**

While many toddlers sleep through the night, at this age, sleep problems can still be expected. And lack of sleep can lead to tantrums and general crankiness in toddlers. Remember that you need up to 14 hours of sleep a day for your toddler, so it is essential that you are sticking to a schedule involving plenty of naps and an early bedtime.

Typically, the toddler stage often entails the transition from sleeping in a crib to sleeping in a large child's bed, but parents should not feel forced at a certain age to make the transfer. If your child feels happy in a cradle, there is generally no need to shift them once they are older. If your child is younger, they might still take two naps a day. Unless you've already begun to see signs that something is changing on its own, you don't need to change that.

For instance, if your child faces trouble falling asleep at what would be the usual time for a nap or doesn't seem exhausted in the morning at the same time, it might be time for only one nap a day. For the afternoon nap, the same is true. If it starts getting later and later, the chances are that you will only get out of the morning nap and then get to an afternoon nap.

For your child to experience longer, more profound, healthier sleep, aim to minimize unplanned naps. If your toddler takes a short rest, it might be easy to tackle the trip in the car, but do your best to keep them alert or schedule the trip for a time when they will not be tired.

Naturally, a nap can arrive at about noon if the toddler wakes at around 8 o'clock. It lasts roughly 2 to 2.5 hours. It will mean that your toddler wakes up at 3 p.m. That's perfect for 7:30 p.m. Time for bed from 7:30 p.m. to sleep towards 8 a.m. It gives about 12.5 hours of sleep at night. Add on the sleep, and you will get to 15 hours of that.

Family schedules would determine differences. Merely adjusting the hours, however, won't always work to alleviate issues. The most important ones are bedtime and wake-up hours. Going to sleep early in the evening coincides with your toddler's natural inner rhythm.

Most families and their toddlers sleep at the same time. There are some benefits to having your child in your bed; there is some evidence that it may disturb everyone's sleep, particularly parents.

- **Safety**

The main factor for the death of children under the age of 4 in the U.S. is accidents. If you follow any simple safety guidelines, many of those accidents can be avoided.

Remember these safety tips:

- **Firearm Hazards:**

If you have a toddler, consider withdrawing weapons from the house. Keep it shot and locked in a secure place if you want to keep a gun. Store the ammunition individually. Ask how arms are kept when your child visits another home or if they attend an in-home daycare.

- **Poisoning:**

By sticking everything in their mouths, toddlers discover. For any harmful household goods and drugs, use safety caps, and keep them out of sight and out of control. Store the poison control number on your phone and post it in your house so that you can quickly find it in the case of an emergency.

- ○ **Burns:**

Toddlers also grasp to steady themselves whatever is around them. Unfortunately, grabbing a hot oven door or pot handle can mean that. The best thing is to keep your little one out of the kitchen while you prepare.

- ○ **Falls:**

Most falls are not a concern, but a severe risk can arise from stairs, sharp-edged furniture, and open windows. For your child to keep him away from the stairs, use gates and mount window guards above the first floor. Do not leave chairs or things that can be used by your child to climb on nearby countertops or tables.

- ○ **Drowning:**

Only 2 inches of water can lead to the drowning of a toddler. Keep the toilet doors locked. Ensure to not leave your child alone in the vicinity of a bathtub, a bucket of water, a swimming or wading pool, or any other water. Stay within your child's arm's reach when you are near water.

- ○ **Car Accidents:**

Toddlers must stay in back-facing car seats until they are two years old or until the height and weight indicated by the safety seat manufacturer is reached. Make sure that the security seats are correctly placed. Never leave your child in or near the vehicle alone.

- • **Technology**

Children under the age of 2 were advised by the American Academy of Pediatrics not to be subjected to screen time. However, in 2016, the policy was revised as more applications and blogs became more child-friendly.

However, for toddlers, screen time can also be used with strict moderation.

Healthy ways of using digital devices include reading books or using apps that allow your little to chat with distant relatives through video.

Try to minimize the amount of TV your child watches and do not keep the TV on for background noise because there is proof that it could affect your child's ability to learn.

 If you think about taking your toddler to the movies, think twice. If you are taking older children to a movie, consider getting your toddler a sitter. Movies can be too noisy for them, and the pictures can be very frightening.

Toddlers want as much of the environment to be experienced as they can. They are always trying to understand everything they can, from how something like a block sounds when it's hit on the floor to how dirt tastes when they put it in their mouth.

Generally, they are only concerned about their own needs because they cannot feel other's situations yet. So, if they don't get their way, your toddler will experience a lot of anger. They will be copying other individuals at this age. They're going to want to try to do the same things at daycare that you do or mimic the other kids.

5.3 Parenting and Your 3 Year Old Kid

To learn what most children can do as they grow, use our developmental milestones.

Your kid at the age of 3 is growing up quickly and can look like a mini-adult walking, talking. The fact that your child is still in pull-ups may be one of the few reminders of his generation. A 3-year-old is beginning to get a better understanding of the universe and how things work within it. His newfound speech and movement abilities are not fully perfected, and tensions will lead to more temper alterations than you are used to, earning him the affectionate title of "three-nager." However, 3 is beautiful age, and the successes of your child will blow you away.

Your preschooler may be learning at three years of age:

- **Understanding Her Bond to Others.**

Your child will begin playing with other kids and, without encouragement, may even start to display affection for friends and family. She may immerse herself in imagination and fantasy and will begin to imitate her parents.

- **Show off New Sets of Skills.**

Your preschooler puts his outstanding problem-solving and fine motor (little muscle) abilities together. He knows how things match and work together.

- Master Emerging Concepts.

Your three-year-old knows concepts such as opposites (big versus small and old versus new), time of day, and things that match.

- **Get Around in Styles.**

Your preschooler continues to develop skills for the gross motor (large muscle). Now she's much less shaky, with fewer falls; she's on to more advanced movements with alternating moves, such as ascending stairs.

- **Have Deeper Discussions.**

At three, your child gets very good at expressing himself. By now, he can know about 250 to 500 words and speak in 5 to 6-word sentences.

It is ca the "terrible 2's," "trusting 3's," and "pleasing 4's," but it can be more challenging than the 2's to have a 3-year-old. You're not alone if you're beginning to feel like you don't like taking care of your 3-year-old.

Here are tips for Parents of 3- year old kids.

- **Avoid Yelling and Show Affection.**

Yelling is a tool for late security, a strategy that we use when anything else fails. But shouting can affect children more than we realize it can cause an immediate behavior change, but it can cause real psychological damage in the long run. Kids need constructive parenting for safe brain growth instead of shouting and harsh punishment.

- **Encourage Better Communication Skills.**

Incredibly vital are the communication abilities of small kids. When they start commuting to a nursery, the stronger their communication skills are, the more comfortable they can deal with other children and teachers.

- **Teach Kids to be Good Listeners.**

We all know that containing the unpredictable mind of a toddler is a challenge. At preschool, however, she will have to participate in different activities such as singing, drawing, listening to her teacher's interpretation, etc. These are all going to require her to sit still and pay attention. Being a good listener will assist her in her nursery to engage proactively in different events.

- **Stay Attuned.**

Attunement, or how well you understand your child's needs at any given moment, is the secret to raising emotionally stable children. In short, tuning is putting yourself in the shoes of your child and then satisfying their needs with a parent's wisdom. Try to find the source of the misbehavior of your child-why she won't put her shoes on or why she's having a tantrum-then customize the impact properly. Most discipline and parenting books revolve around the same themes-be consistent, follow-through with implications, don't send too many reminders, do not punish in frustration, etc. While I agree with these themes, there is a danger of being too formulaic. In parenting attunement, we don't just give time-out as a rote reaction to wrongdoing. "Attuned parents, instead, ask" why "a child is misbehaving. We will help address their needs, value them, and get long-term healthy habits when recognizing the origin of a child's misbehavior.

- **Give Attention to Your Kids Frequently in Small Doses.**

This one is for you if your 3-year-old takes your mobile phone out of your hands, hits your keyboard as you write, or knocks on piles of laundry. I know your 3-year-old needs your full attention all the time, but if you are trying to do laundry, run errands, read your email, or have a life, that's not possible. So when you know that your sweet baby is trying to get your attention, give her full attention for a few seconds. Look into her eyes right now, ask her a few questions, and listen to her answer. You can use attention-showing body language, like putting down your phone. Please think of how you are going to redirect her when you listen to her responses.

- **Redirect with Activity.**

Try early, and with a loving expression, to redirect. Tell yourself, "Why does my child misbehave?" Really, what do they need? "Typically, offensive actions involve physical redirection. For instance, they may need to ride a bike outside if a child is snatching toys or screaming. If a child lies and whines on the floor, they may need a little love and some quiet activity. Try reading a book for them.

- **Anticipate Repeat Offenders.**

Kids have habits of misbehavior, like adults. Time and again, they do the same bad things. Are you battling every morning over clothing, or are you struggling to get your 3-year-old packed into her car seat? Know your repeated crimes, intervene early, and empower your child to make the right decisions. I had a 3-year-old who liked to refuse to get strapped into her car seat because she knew she could manipulate the entire family. Once she was strapped in, the car would not move. The more she resisted, the angrier our other kids got, and she felt dominant. "So one day, on my way to my car, I said, "If everybody says, 'We love you, we love you! 'Three times, are you going to strap on the car seat and be happy? She said, "OK, but five times you have to repeat it." We did it, strapped it in, and everyone laughed at it.

- **Set Some Expectations.**

Write the family rules list. Make a list short and easy for 3-year-olds.

For instance

- Use loving voices
- Obey Mommy and Daddy
- Do not harm others.

Discuss the rules regularly, and celebrate dinner or bedtime accomplishments.

- **Teach Obedience.**

Children are not born obedient, and we need to teach them. Naturally, 3-year-olds are seeking individuality and will combat obedience. The trick is to teach children that they want to be obedient when they do, as you say, they get plenty of praise and positive reinforcement. Play "Simon Says" to practice obedience, except to change it to "Mommy Says," or, "Daddy Says." Start with everyday things such as patting your head and clapping your hands, then move to put away toys.

- **Use a Behavior Sticker Chart.**

Stickers are never going to be as strong again when your child is 3. Enjoy yourself. Get a sticker chart, and start recording the days that your 3-year-old stayed in bed, washed her plate, kept her underwear dry all day long, etc.

- **Stay Consistent.**

Consistency does not imply excessive penalties or shouting; it means treating the same problem habits regularly. If it's not OK on Monday to leave your shoes on the floor, you can't pick them up on Tuesday for your boy. That doesn't mean your 3-year-old requires a verbal lashing.

- **Get on the Same Page with Childcare Providers.**

What are constructive incentive mechanisms in effect in the room of your child's nursery? What about the House of Grandma? Try them at home, too, if they work outside the house. The laws ought to be as close as possible at school and home.

There are more tips for better management of your kids' behaviors and make them feel confident. In the coming chapter, we will discuss helpful techniques for parents of kids above age four. These will help you better monitor kids and polish their skills to make them an emotionally intelligent.

5.4 Parenting Tips for 4-5 Years Kids

The Wonder Years were called for three to five years of age, and they are fantastic, ping-ponging from optimism to crying, from tantrums to cuddling, from belief in fairy tales to intellectual strides that are mind-boggling.

Explorers, researchers, artists, and experimenters are preschoolers. They are experiential learners, but to figure out what's reliable, they want to reach boundaries. They learn how to make friends, communicate with the world, and regulate their bodies, feelings, and minds. These years will provide a stable and limitless base for your son or daughter's entire childhood, with a little support from you.

- **Structure.**

Daily routines help children feel safe and are vital for preschoolers who grapple with big fears daily. The world is unpredictable and terrifying to them; they should be predictable in their home. With regular meals and bedtime rituals, a calm, tidy, and enjoyable environment can create happy children who have the inner tools to meet every day developmental challenges. No, that doesn't mean that you're going to have to be rigid. But there is a need for your child to know what to expect.

- **Enough Sleep**

Preschoolers may avoid bedtime, but three to five-year-olds do not have the resourcefulness to cope with the demands of their day without adequate sleep. Establish a daily routine that allows her to wind down and begin to relax long before bedtime. Indeed, he still gets some time to relax every day when he gives up his nap.

- **Nutrition:**

You decide what food in your house is accessible, but your child's responsibility is to determine how much she eats. Bear in mind that kids need regular small meals, and they'll end up snacking all day if you don't have that. You will feel relaxed, letting them pick which foods they consume and how much if you always have a variety of healthy foods.

A picky eater worried? Serve a menu of nutritious foods to prevent power struggles; as her taste buds grow, your child will slowly widen her choices. As long as there are no sweets available (except as occasional not regular treats), preschoolers will naturally prefer healthier foods that suit their physical needs over some time. You do not require to make a clean plate as the target; instead, ask them how their body feels when they say they're done. If you're worried about throwing the food away, ask yourself why not wasting, food is more important than the potential physical health and body image of your child? (Obesity starts in pre-school!)

- **Help with Emotions.**

Although your child may no longer have frequent tantrums, he still has excellent emotions, and he still needs you to always "listen" to those emotions. To vent the anxieties that eventually build up in a small person fighting to handle herself in a vast, sometimes daunting world, all kids need regular laughter, so be sure to build regular roughhousing into your schedule.

And occasionally, you can expect your preschooler to communicate his needs as an attack, suggesting that a suffering child can well scream, "I hate you; I want a new mom!" Don't take it personally. Instead, even when you set boundaries, empathize. "You've got to be so mad about talking to me like that ... I think you're upset ... you wanted to, and I said no ... I am sorry, Sweetie, this is so hard."

- **Empathetic Limits.**

Resist every temptation to punish if you want well-behaved kids. Kids of this age need guide and limits, as they are actively learning the rules and how the world works, and they will test naturally to see just where those limits are. Remember, though, that they're still developing their brains. They get flooded very quickly with emotion. They get upset when you set boundaries, partly because they want what they want, but partly because they are worried about your disapproval. When you empathize with their disappointment or anger, it helps them to calm themselves. Doing so will help them learn to control their feelings over time and maintain their balance as they get older in the face of upsets. Research demonstrates that their behavior worsens when young kids are punished. Instead, set boundaries and empathize with emotions to make your child WANT to act. Instead of depending on you to regulate him, this helps him develop self-discipline.

- **Interaction Time with Parents**

Your preschooler's brain, both in learning facts and in learning emotional self-regulation, is experiencing rapid growth and consolidation. For your preschooler's mental and even brain growth, most of the intimate time with physically and emotionally affectionate parents is essential. It suggests what psychologists call "Floor Time," which gets down to its level to work together to create the train or tower track. The argument is not the building's intellectual work, but the emotional bond you develop over it and the caring help you provide when the project inevitably runs into snags. Your relationship will be built on a regular, unstructured "special time" with your child during which you let your child take the lead. Instead, give your child "Cozy Time" if you can't bear one more superhero or dollhouse game. Only snuggle up for a lazy half hour on the couch with a pile of books, and ensure you take plenty of time out to talk about what you're reading or about your day.

- **Hear Your Kids Questions.**

From the constant "WHY?" to badgering parents to change their minds about a cap, preschoolers are famous for asking questions. If you look below the surface at the query's reason, this can make a parent insane. Your child wants a lot of information; he wants to be understood, to be noticed, to tell you what he feels, with your guidance. He wants to weave his world view together and to have you react to the overwhelming emotions that sometimes threaten to overpower his developing intellectual control. When your kid devastates you on WHY? Questions and your responses do not seem satisfied, so she keeps asking, flipping it around and asking her the question.

- ○ **Help Your Kid to Express Himself without Whining.**

Whining can propel the crazy of even the most patient parent. But whining is an indication that your child needs support, either in processing feelings that weigh on her or meeting other needs. She's not only trying to get her way; by asserting some power, she communicates the need for all preschoolers to begin to master their world.

- • **Social Time**

Biologically, preschoolers are designed to look up to older children. Young kids are old enough to leave the parent tag with the big kids and learn social skills in the tribal cultures that are natural to humans. Since our children are typically in groups of peers of the same age, to learn to take turns or refrain from bossiness, they also require adult assistance and modeling. Four-year-olds are experimenting with the correct use of force, so they are known for bossiness and even intimidation. Don't feel guilty for stepping in to model healthy social activity in the playground. How else should they learn?

Skills are called developmental milestones, such as naming colors, showing affection, and hopping on one foot. Developmental milestones are stuff that most kids at a certain age will do. Children achieve milestones in how they (like crawling, walking, or jumping) play, learn, talk, act, and travel.

- ○ When children grow into early childhood, their world will begin to open up. They will become more autonomous and start focusing more on adults and children outside the family.

- ○ Kids want to explore and to ask even more about the things around them. They will help shape their personality and their ways of thinking and moving through their interactions with family and those around them.

- ○ Children can ride a tricycle during this stage, use safety scissors, notice a distinction between girls and boys, help dress and undress themselves, play with other kids, remember part of a story, and sing a song.

- **Child Safety**

You and your child must be aware of ways to remain healthy when your child is more independent and enjoys more time in the outside world. To protect your child, here are a few tips:

Tell your child why staying out of traffic is essential. Tell him not to play or run after stray balls in the street.

When letting your child ride their tricycle, be careful. Keep her away from the street and on the sidewalk and still make her wear a helmet.

- **Healthy Bodies:**

- ○ Whenever possible, eat meals with your kids. Let your child see you enjoying your meals and snacks with fruit, vegetables, and whole grains. Only a small amount of food and beverages containing added sugars, solid fats, or salt should be eaten and drunk by your child.

- ○ Keep the TV sets in your child's bedroom. Set screen time limits for your child to no more than 1 hour of quality programming per day, at home, school, or after-school care, and develop a family media use plan.

- ○ Provide age-appropriate play equipment for your kids, such as balls and plastic bats, but let your preschooler pick what to play with. For your preschooler, this makes moving and being actively enjoyable.

- Be sure your child gets the suggested amount of sleep every night: 10-13 hours every 24 hours (including naps) for preschoolers 3-5 years old.

5.5 Whining of Kids and How to Stop?

By whining, should children get what they want? Certainly not.

Do they know that by conveying good arguments and making them logical, funny, charming in a better way for your needs and theirs, they can get their way? If you want them in life to get anywhere.

But how will the transformation help them make it?

With toddlers and preschoolers, crying is normal. Parents commonly recommend telling their children to ask in a "sweet" voice, so they cannot hear the whiny voice. But moaning is symptomatic of a deeper issue. So, if you want to eradicate moaning, you need to tackle what's behind it.

If the moaning of your child drives you nuts, six parent-proven secrets are here to stop the moaning. What secret you're using depends on why he whines?

- **Whining because He has no Internal Tools to Deal with What is being Demanded of Him.**

When humans feel overwhelmed, they get whiny. (He may have thrown himself howling to the ground like a toddler, but instead of three or four, he will always cry and complain.) Satisfy his basic food needs, rest, downtime, run-around time, and interaction with you, or you can count on moaning. He might not want to a tantrum as much as he used to, but if you force him to endure the shopping trip when hungry and exhausted, he will complain. Why build a stressful situation that stresses both of you and adds to the moaning habit?

- **The Kid is Whining Because She Needs More Attention.**

Become pre-emptive. Make sure your child gets enough of your optimistic, unjustified attention. Minimize whining Until she becomes demanding by paying attention. Anyone who has had to ask, "Do you love me?" to a romantic partner knows the given after you ask can never really satisfy the need. The tip is to take the initiative and give attention to the child hasn't asked for, always, so she feels your love and engagement.

And, of course, when she shows the first sign of needing your emotional support, it's especially important to communicate before that fast downhill slide. No, by paying her attention when she's whining, you're not rewarding "evil" actions. If she was crying from hunger, would you think you were rewarding it by feeding her? It is our responsibility to fulfill children's needs, so they have the internal resources to deal with it. Communication is a basic human need, and without it, children will not work well.

- **Whining Because She Doesn't Like What IS Going on, But Feels Afraid of Finding Her Way:**

The author of the wonderful book Playful Parenting, Lawrence Cohen, says:

When children cry, they are feeling powerless. If we admonish them for whining or refuse to listen to them, we increase their powerlessness feelings. If we do not say anything so they will stop whining, we reward that powerlessness. But if we calmly, playfully, communicate with them to use a strong voice, we enhance their sense of self-esteem and competence. And we find a Passover back to close the connection.

Remember, you're out to connect, not to manipulate her. Start by letting her know you hear what she needs, and you're seeing her point of view: You want to go to the playground, and you keep telling me that, and here I keep stopping at all those stores you don't expect, and you're frustrated, right? Sometimes it's enough to feel understood to stop whining in her tracks.

"Then you might playfully say," You don't sound like yourself if she keeps complaining. I wonder where your familiar powerful voice has gone?

Express faith that your child can use her "solid" voice and give your support by turning it into a game to help her find it:

"Hey, where was your strong voice going? A minute ago, it was here. I LOVE your strong voice! I'm going to help you find it. Help me look. Is it under the chair? No behind the door? No, HEY! You found it!! That was your strong voice!! Yay! I love your strong voice! Now, in your strong voice, tell me again what you need."

Finally, by teaching her how to ask for something appropriately, and negotiate with you, give her alternate tools. Since whining is so often a basis of powerlessness, it will carry over into the rest of her life to help your child feel that she can get what she wants through reasonable measures.

In other words, you are not letting her learn that by crying or making tantrums, she gets her way in life, but you want her to understand that by controlling her feelings, viewing it from the other person, and setting up win/win scenarios, she can get what she wants. (And that is what you always try to model, of course.)

But if you don't have time today to go to the playground, don't do it. Be empathic with your kid's desire, and nurture him through the meltdown. But if your objection is whining, she manages to pull herself and ask what she wants reasonably. You can drive to engage in the kind of conflict resolution that finds a win/win solution.

Do you reward whining? No, you are encouraging him by showing that the way to get what he wants in life is to find options that work for both of you. I often listen to parents saying that this "empowering with the strong voice game" strategy works like magic the first time or two, but the child ignores to play after that.

- **Sometimes kid Whines Because He Wants to Cry.**

He has many pent-up feelings about things that stress him the new babysitter you left him with on Friday night, the kid who grabbed the sandbox truck, potty training, the new baby there is no end to stressful developmental challenges! Toddlers let off stress by only having a meltdown, but they gain more self-control as they get older, and instead start whining. In response to his whining, be kind until you get home and have to spend a few minutes with him. Pull him up on your lap, look him in the eye, and say,

"I notice you felt so whiny and sad, Sweetie. Do you have to cuddle and cry a bit, maybe? Sometimes everyone needs to cry. I'm right here to hold you."

- **Kids Whine Because It Works.**

Do not give a whining reward, meaning don't break in and buy the candy. There is never, however, a reason for being less than kind about it. Responding with empathy to his desire ("You are so sad that I said no; you want to have that candy) helps him with his disappointment to feel less lonely. And there's nothing wrong with discovering something else, like a shiny red apple or a trip to the playground, that will make him happy. It teaches him to look for win/win approach and propose them. If, on the other side, he thinks that by moaning, he gets what he wants, he can become an expert whiner.

- **Kids Whine Because You Will Do Anything to Stop It.**

Why is it that parents hate whining so much? Because whining is the more mature form of crying for your little one. She makes you know that she needs your attention. And human adults are conditioned to respond as often to moaning as we do to screaming, so tiny people's needs are met. So you respond with anxiety the minute you hear that whine. To stop it, you'll do anything.

But if you can take some pause and remember that there's no emergency, you're going to feel a lot better, and you're going to be a better parent. Don't let your fight or flight kick in with your automatic crisis mode. Don't feel like you have to fix the problem, or do anything but love your child at all. Give a smile to your child and give her a big hug. The whining would end most of the time.

Chapter 6: Positive Parenting Tips for Kids Above Six Years Age

School-age children are packets of busy energy. Their personalities are straightforward, and some separate interests and talents are created. Knowing your school-age child's needs can ensure that you're helping him stay as healthy as possible so he can be at his best. These strategies can also assist you in instilling your child with lifelong healthy habits.

6.1 Best Piece of Advices for Raising Happy, and Healthy School Age Kids

In many areas of life, including her grooming habits, your school-age child is likely to be very independent. She is expected to shower, but she may need some supervision to confirm she removes shampoo from her hair.

Likewise, your school-age child should have the motor skills to brush her teeth that she wants. But, to brush longer, she may need some support or need some supervision when it comes to flossing. Although some school-age children are reasonably consistent with taking care of their bodies, others may need a little extra help.

- **Nutrition**

Grade-schoolers are extremely smart about eating. The boy who once swallowed every sprout of Brussels set before him may suddenly swear that he hates them. With her afternoon snack, the girl was always perfectly happy to drink water may start begging for soda. The chances are that these sudden appetite changes have less to do with your kid's taste buds and more to do with a desire to fit in with his peers.

- For ensuring that your child is adequately nourished, here are some things that you can do: Stock the house with only safe options. Make it easy to see and reach your child with fruit, veggies, yogurt, milk, and cheese.

- Before a meal, restrict liquids. Before meals, discourage your kid from filling up on milk or juice. He will not feel much like eating solid food if his tummy is full of fluid.

- Make your meals as happy as possible. If your kid is not hungry, don't try to make your child eat, or push him to eat anything he doesn't like. And when you want him to do something or punish him for not eating, never use food as a bribe or reward. Steer the table talk on friendly subjects; save his teacher's discussion of that note for after dinner.

- Offer your kid some freedom. Even if he asks every day for the same ham sandwich in his lunchbox or the only green thing he'll come close to is broccoli, you don't have to overthink what he's eating, as long as he has plenty of energy and usually develops. Most children do not eat a healthy diet every day, but they will manage to get the full range of nutrients over a week. If you are very concerned about your infant's nutrition, a pediatrician's check-in should put your mind at ease.

- Set a good example. Maybe your big kid boy, but your child is always looking for guidance from you. Eat as you want him to eat, in other words. Even if he is not following suit at the moment, your decisions will affect him.

- For an occasional treat, present sweets. Daily, stop serving high-calorie, sugary snacks. Every night after dinner, your child does not need a sweet dessert and do not give him cookies, cakes, or candy for school.

- When you find he is not eating well, you might consider giving your child a daily vitamin, although most kids do not need it.

- **Physical Health**

Every day, kids need about twice as much physical activity as adults need.

- Healthy aerobic exercises for kids, maybe biking, playing soccer, or riding a bicycle. Activities for muscle strengthening are also significant. A couple of tasks that improve their muscles are crossing the monkey bars on the playground or climbing trees.

- Basketball, tennis, biking, jumping rope, or games such as hop-scotch may be effective ways to strengthen their bones. School-age children can also engage in bone-building activities.

- Break time, gym class, and sports activities can count towards the recommendation for your child's physical activity, but it may not be enough. Include physical activity into your life as a family. After dinner, go for a family walk, take hikes on weekends, or go swimming together as a family. You can also like to play catch, go to an obstacle course, or kick a ball together. Your child can develop healthy behaviors from watching you, so when it comes to physical activity, make sure you are a successful role model.

- **Around the House:**

Many school-age children are willing to take on some duties of their own. When your child already makes his bed and keeps his room tidy, he would probably welcome some more "grown-up" age-appropriate tasks, such as being emptier in the designated dishwasher or being responsible for recycling.

Come up with various choices for him to choose from, if you can. He would be more likely to follow through on doing something that he has selected.

Typically, paying a kid for doing chores that are part of being a good citizen, like cleaning up in his room, is not a great idea. It is easier to consider his contribution to family teamwork by his housework. Praise his hard labor and effort. Positive reinforcement would improve his self-esteem and help him to stick with it.

A perfect way to start educating a child about money at 7 or 8 years old, though, is by giving him an allowance. It doesn't matter how much, but one fair way to measure the weekly stipend is to provide him with a half dollar to a whole dollar every year of age, for a 7-year-old between $3.50 and $7. Your child will learn the worth of money and the importance of saving by handling even this small sum.

Your child will always be excited at this age to spend time together as a family. Including a family game night to a pizza time, he might be open to doing just about everything with you. It is the best time to introduce your child to several activities, from baseball games to camping trips. Family activities will teach your child about themselves and give you the chance to create a strong bond.

- **Mental Health**

During the school-age years, mental health problems may develop or become apparent. Children may become depressed or anxious, or they may show signs of behavioral disorders or ADHD. Speak to your pediatrician if you have questions about the mood or actions of your infant. The results of treatment can be improved by early intervention.

- **Sleep:**

Bedtimes are perfect for children in this age group. So while your child may claim that his friends stay up until 9 p.m., you may still give your child 7:30 p.m. Time for bed. But if your child goes to bed earlier than his peers, don't feel guilty. Sleep is essential for the health and growth of your child.

If your child finds difficulty to wake up in the morning, has trouble staying awake in the afternoon, or seems too emotional, maybe she's not getting enough rest. Build a schedule for your child's bedtime. A few hours before she sleeps, please turn off all devices and consider any other disturbances that may interfere with her sleep. Encourage her to read books or, before going to bed, indulge in some peaceful activities.

- **Safety:**

Grade school is an excellent time to help a child learn to be vigilant about their safety.

- **Teaching Street Smarts:**

Until crossing, for example, remind your child to look at both directions more than once. Go over what he can do if a stranger confronts him.

  - Make sure that he doesn't know how to get into a car with someone he doesn't know, even if that person says that you said it'd be all right.

  - Speak to your child about what to do in an emergency. Ensure that your child knows how to call emergency number, what constitutes an emergency, and what the dispatcher may say. Accidents are the biggest danger at this age that your child is likely to face. These techniques will decrease the risk of death or injury to your child.

  - Do not ditch the seat for the booster. A child who is itching to claim his autonomy may beg to stop using one. However, unless your child is impressive for his age, don't give in. The American Academy of Pediatrics told that car accidents are the leading cause of death among children. The best way for keeping a child safe in the car is to keep him in a booster seat unless he is at least 4 feet, 9 inches tall, a height that most children do not reach till they are between 8 and 12.

- **Implement Safe Play.**

It means ensuring that your child uses any safety equipment needed for the activity he's doing. For example, he must wear a helmet that suits if he's biking. Dream of lessons if he can't swim yet.

- ○ **Insist on Proper Facilities for Sports.** Ensure you have the right gear, such as a mouth guard, helmet, and knee pads, if your child is playing a sport. Make sure that his machinery suits correctly and learn about the symptoms of a concussion.

- • **Technology:**

Your school-age child may demonstrate an interest in the internet. Some of his friends might also have smartphones or tablets of their own, or they might talk about social media.

While there's nothing wrong with kids enjoying technology under an adult's watchful eye, the internet can be risky for kids who lack supervision. There is a lot of stuff young kids shouldn't be exposed to, from adult video games to online predators. But, there are also other hidden risks, such as marketers of junk food who sell their material online to kids.

- ○ For children, high-quality programming may be educational. But, it can be detrimental to get too much screen time. They alert parents not to allow screen time to interfere with proper sleep, physical activity, and other health-critical behaviors.

- ○ Approve any video games and movies that your child needs to watch and know what he may have access to in the homes of his peers. He is using parental controls, too.

- ○ Set safe screen time limits, too. Don't encourage your child in the bedroom to have a TV and don't encourage him to play video games on an unlimited basis.

- ○ Too much sedentary exercise is not ideal for his physical health, in addition to taking a toll on his psychological well-being. So allow your kid to spend a lot of time playing outdoors or interacting with his friends in face-to-face experiences.

- **World of Your School-Age Child:**

When kids mature, school work becomes more difficult. So this is when some children start to flourish, and others struggle to grasp more sophisticated concepts. Homework can be a significant struggle for many families. Many school-age children hesitate to sit down and prepare or complete their math homework for a spelling test.

- Sports, music, and after-school events are busy for many kids. However, some would choose to spend endless hours on their digital devices. At this age, it's crucial to keep children mentally and physically active.
- During this time, too, friends become a bigger deal. Helping your child to see colleagues outside of school is a smart idea. It can be beneficial for their growth to attend birthday parties or play on the playground with children.

- Bullying can become an issue at this age. It's important to talk about kindness and respect with your child so that he doesn't become a bully, and if he becomes a victim, it's also imperative that you talk about what he can do.

6.2 Your Tweens and Some Parenting Tips

The intermediate years are an era of transformation. Maturity levels differ significantly at this age, not just a little kid, but not quite a teenager. It is appropriate to teach children the life skills they will need to succeed in the teenage years and beyond.

- **Daily Life:**

Lots of tweens are pretty autonomous. With little reminders, they can take care of their hygiene, do their chores, and complete their homework. Others need a little extra help, however. It's a good idea to start helping them become more accountable to take care of their health and well-being if your child is not inspired to get things done on their own.

- **Nutrition:**

The nutrition of your child is vital to their overall health. Consuming three meals a day and two nutritious snacks should be part of proper nutrition.

Limit high levels of sugar and foods high in fat. And encourage your child to consume plenty of fruits, vegetables, lean meats, and milk products that are low in fat. For helping the tween grow to its full potential, a healthy diet is necessary.

For tweens, it's natural to experience appetite fluctuations. A rise in appetite can lead to growth spurts. For keeping your child safe, the best nutrition advice includes urging them to:

- Eating a range of foods.
- Balancing the food, you consume with physical activity

- ○ Consume plenty of grain products, fruits, and vegetables
- ○ Choose fat, saturated fat, and cholesterol-low foods.
- ○ Consume in moderation with sugar and salt
- ○ Consuming enough calcium and iron to fulfill the requirements of their growing body

With low-fat meals, low-calorie and snacks, and desserts, full your kitchen. Enable only low fat or skim milk to drink your tween. Keep as much as possible out of the house with high-calorie snacks, such as chips, soft drinks, or ice cream.

Enjoy your dinner together as a family, and let everyone enjoy their meals. Don't argue at the dinner table about homework or other problems. Keep the talk as fun as possible, instead.

Don't push a tween to eat something that he doesn't want. Offer dinner with nutritious meals, and if he's hungry, he'll eat it. If he doesn't like what you're serving, you don't need to make a separate meal for your boy.

Don't use food for your tween bribe or incentive. Even if your growing adolescents are picky eaters, don't make a big deal of their eating habits. Focusing too much on it will make matters worse.

For moderately active boys, the suggested calories include:

- ○ 10 years: 1,800 calories / day
- ○ 11 years: 2,000 calories / day
- ○ 12 years: 2.200 calories / day

For moderately active girls, the recommended calories include:

- ○ 10 years: 1,800 calories / day
- ○ 11 years: 1,800 calories / day
- ○ 12 years: 2,000 calories / day

Moderately active means an intermediate that engages in physical activity of at least 60 minutes, at least five days a week. Less active tweens should consume fewer calories, and more active tweens may need more.

- **Physical Activity for Your Tweens:**

Tweens are urged to get at least 60 minutes of physical activity every day. Because many of them no longer have recess, making sure you emphasize physical activity at home becomes more important than ever.

- ○ Aerobic exercise should be used in all of their physical activity. The aerobic activities you might enjoy are playing sports, riding a bike, or jogging.

- ○ Activities for muscle strengthening are also significant. In lifting weights or doing strength training exercises, some tweens can show interest.
- ○ Bone building activities should also involve tweens. Basketball, rope jumping, or running will all help to create bones.

- ○ Include physical activity into your life as a family. You can Go for a family walk in the evenings, play a sport together, or go on weekends for long bike rides.

- ○ You can enjoy playing catch, heading to a barrier course, or kicking a ball together. Your child can develop healthy behaviors from watching you, so when it comes to physical activity, make sure you are a successful role model.

- ○ In the twilight years, body image disorders are prevalent. So, rather than losing weight or looking better, it's essential to emphasize exercising to stay healthy and build strong bones.

- **Around the House:**

Tweens enjoy spending more and more time hanging out with friends with their friends. Although they're still interested in family time, they might be willing to ditch their family plans if a friend calls. However, that doesn't mean you can give up on fun family nights. Your tween may appreciate a particular time with you. If you play board games, engage in physical activity, or discover new areas, it can be fun to connect by doing exercise together.

  - At times, your tween may even become rude and need discipline. They might insist that they know everything or say that, according to her terms, they will do their chores. Their way of achieving some freedom is to try to assert themselves. By giving them two options, you can provide them with an opportunity to build autonomy. Ask, "Want to clean your room before or after dinner?" Just make sure, with either option, you can live.

  - Tweens need to have the skills to perform most household tasks. Ensure you cover safety precautions if you're going to encourage your tween to use household chemicals or do some cooking.

  - Making space in the dishwasher, washing windows, cleaning floors, vacuuming, and cleaning the bathroom may be sufficient chores.

  - A chore chart could be an excellent way to remind you of what you want from them. It will decrease the desire to nag them or ask them always to do the chores.

  - Whether she's acting professionally, give benefits, and rewards. You may equate their duties with rights, such as screen time, or you may provide an allowance.

- **Health and Safety:**

For brief periods, your child can be ready to stay home alone. But before you suggest leaving your tween alone, make sure you know your state or local laws.

- ○ Also, some tweens might not be relaxed without adult guidance, so know whether or not your tween is ready for the experience before you test the waters.

- ○ Your baby is old enough to think about basic first aid now. Treat superficial cuts and bruises, brace your tween, and instruct your tween to use the different things in your family's first aid kit.

- ○ Your local hospital can also provide first aid and CPR classes for tweens and teenagers. Consider taking your tween to a level so that you are both ready for those emergencies.

- **Visit the Doctor:**

Yearly wellness appointments with the pediatrician are recommended unless your tween has health concerns.

You may expect: at your tween's annual checkup:

- ○ An analysis of the growth and development of your child

- ○ An analysis of routines for diet and sleep
- ○ Their height, weight, and blood pressure measurements
- ○ Injury prevention therapy, oral hygiene, and a healthy diet
- ○ An analysis of results in schools
- ○ Immunizations: tetanus booster (Tdap), meningococcal and HPV (boys and girls) vaccinations, and possibly others
- ○ Vision test screening
- ○ Common health concerns in tweens are similar to younger kids. At this age, respiratory infections and constipation may be issued. For puberty issues, tweens can even see a doctor. In tweens who begin puberty, acne can begin.

- Also, gynecomastia can be a concern. As your children are going through puberty, it is not rare for boys to have some breast growth. It usually starts as a slight bump, which may be tender, under one or both nipples. Without medication, you should inform your child that this breast lump is natural and should disappear within a few months or years.
- Injuries associated with sports are expected at this age, too. The consequence of a series of physical activities can be sprains, broken bones, or bruises.

- **Physical Activity:**

A lot of your tween time can be filled by extracurricular sports, homework, family time, friends, and electronics. Sleep deprivation will take its toll if they eat into your child's rest time.

- To ensure that your child has ample sleep time, you will have to take note of how much sleep your child is having and then change your child's routine accordingly.

- Before hitting the bed, make sure your tween has time to cool down from his or her day. Listening to the music, reading, or taking a hot shower before bed may involve calming down activities.

- It might be a sign that she's not getting enough sleep if your tween has trouble waking up in the morning or she's having trouble staying up during the day.

- **Safety:**

Accidents are a major of infant mortality. Most of these fatalities could easily be avoided; it is essential always to have your child's welfare in mind.

Here are some healthy tips for keeping your tween:

- If required, keep your tween in a booster seat. When your tween exceeds the weight and height harness strap limits of their forward-facing car seat, older school-age children can sit in a belt-positioning booster seat. The AAP suggests that children not use an adult seatbelt until they are between 8 and 12 years old and are 4 feet 9 inches in height.

- In the backseat, your child can ride. Children below 13 years of age can sit in the car's back seat. Do not let your child ride in a pickup truck's cargo area, even if it is enclosed. Kids in the back of a pickup truck have no protection from severe injury or death in an accident.

- Insist on safety devices. Teach your child always to wear all of the appropriate protective equipment (helmets, mouth guards, pads, etc.) made for each sport.

- You are teaching safety on bicycles. Without a helmet, do not let your child ride a bike. You are teaching public safety laws, intersections, and sidewalks.

- Practice food security. Do not eat undercooked meat or poultry, drink unpasteurized milk or juices, or wash fruits and vegetables.\

- Mount alarms for smoke and carbon monoxide. In a fire at home, have an evacuation plan, use flame retardant sleepwear and educate your child about fire protection (never play games, etc.).

- o Safely store guns. If a weapon has to be kept in the building, keep it secured. Keep it unloaded and keep the ammunition individually stored. Speak to your interviewer about the safety of firearms.

- o Teach your child how the emergency number should be dialed. Make sure you know what an emergency is and how to call for help.
- o It's also necessary to start talking about social problems, such as alcohol, drugs, and sex with your tween. While you might believe that your child will never participate in such adult behavior, some of their peers are likely to be good.

- o Tweens must know how to cope with peer pressure and when they experience them, to identify dangers.

- **Technology**

The majority of tweens use electronics to feel relaxed. But do not leave your children unattended.

- o Most teens use social media, have their smartphones, and use the internet daily. And while games, blogs, and apps are available to provide educational material, digital devices can also present tweens with a lot of risks.

- o The world of the web can be unsafe for young people, from cyberbullies to online predators. It is possible that tweens surf the web without adult supervision would come across adult content.

- o Sexting can also become a concern in the twilight years. If your tween asks someone else to see inappropriate images, or your kid is the one who sends nude material, many young people use their mobile devices to share pictures.

- o Set simple rules that will protect the privacy of your tween. Tell your child that revealing their current location, home address (or the address of someone else), social security number, or family members' names is never OK.

- ○ You can choose a nickname instead of their real name if you encourage your child to use social media. Before allowing your child to participate, study the possible risks and benefits of every social networking platform.

- ○ If she ever receives messages that make her feel insecure or comes across offensive material, clarify what your child can do. You can request for her to come to you and tell you what happened.

- ○ In a common area of the house, make your interview use their digital devices. Often, you peek over her shoulder so that you know what she's doing—using parental controls to ensure that kid-friendly content is only available to her.

6.3 Young Teens (12-14 Years Age) and Positive Parenting Tips

It is an era of many shifts in physical, mental, emotional, and social conditions. When puberty starts, hormones alter. The majority of boys grow facial and pubic hair, deepening their voices. Many girls develop pubic hair and breasts, and their time starts. They may be concerned about these modifications and how others look at them. It will also be a time when your teen may face social pressure to use alcohol, narcotics, and tobacco products, and to have sex. Eating disorders, depression, and family conflicts may be other obstacles. Teens make more of their own decisions about friends, sports, learning, and school at this age. With their personality and desires, they become more autonomous, while parents are still critical.

- **Emotional / Social Transitions**

In this age group, children might:

- Display more care about the image, appearance, and clothing of the body.
- Rely on themselves; between high expectations and lack of trust, going back and forth.
- Experience a greater moodiness.
- Display more peer group participation and power.

- Express less love for parents; it can seem disrespectful or short-tempered often.
- They are feeling tension from more stressful school assignments.
- Developing issues with eating.
- Feel a lot of sadness or depression, leading to low school grades, use of drugs or alcohol, unsafe sex, and other issues.

- **Young Teenagers Thinking and Learning**

In this age group, children might:

- Have tremendous potential for complex thinking.
- Be better able, by speaking, to convey feelings.
- Create a clearer understanding of right and wrong.
- Tips on Good Parenting

The following are some things that you, as a parent, can do during this period to support your child:

- When thinking about sensitive subjects such as drugs, alcohol, smoking, and sex, be frank and straightforward with your teenager.
- Meet and get to know your peers as a teenager.
- Show an interest in the school life of a teenager.
- Help your teen make the right decisions while promoting him to make his own choices.
- Respect the views of your teenager and take her thoughts and feelings into account. She needs to know that you're listening to her.
- Be clear about goals and expectations when there is a disagreement (such as having good grades, keeping things clean, and showing respect), but give your teen guidance on achieving those goals (such as when and how to study or clean).

6.4 Positive Parenting for Your Teenagers

It is a time of transition in how adolescents think, feel, and connect with others, and how their bodies grow. By now, most girls will be mature mentally, and most will have undergone puberty. During this time, boys could still mature physically. Your teen could have questions about the scale, shape, or weight of her body. Eating disorders, especially among girls, may also be typical.

Your teen is creating his distinctive personality and thoughts during this time. Relationships with friends are still vital, but as he develops a more defined sense of who he is, your teen may have other interests. It is also critical to plan for more freedom and accountability; many teens begin to work, and shortly after high school, many will leave home.

- **Social and Emotional Changes:**

In this age group, children might:

- Have more curiosity and desire in intimate relationships.
- Go through fewer parent disputes.
- Show more parental independence.
- Have a greater desire to care and share and to build more personal relationships.
- Spend less time with family members and more time with family members.
- Feel a great deal of sadness or depression that can lead to low

school grades, use of alcohol or drugs, unsafe sex, and other issues.

- **Thinking and Learning**

In this age group, children might:

- Learn more established habits for work.
- Display more concern about future plans for school and job.
- Be better able to give explanations, like what is right or wrong, for your own decisions.

- **What Can Parents Do for Teenagers?**

- Talk about her issues with your teen and pay attention to any improvements in her behavior. Ask her if, mainly, if she seems sad or depressed, she has had suicidal thoughts. It won't cause her to have suicidal thoughts when asked about these thoughts, but it will help her know that you care about how she feels. If required, seek professional support.

- Show interest in your teenager's school and extracurricular interests and hobbies and encourage him to be involved in activities such as athletics, music, theatre, and painting.

- Encourage your teen to volunteer in her community and get active in civic events.

- Compliment and celebrate your teen and his efforts and achievements.
- Display your teenage love. Spending time together doing stuff you love.

- Value the opinion of your teen. Without playing down her fears, listen to her.

- Motivate your child to share solutions to problems or disputes. Support learn to make responsible choices for your teenager. Develop opportunities and be available for guidance and help for him to use his judgment.

- If your teen is interested in interactive internet media, such as sports, chat rooms, and instant messaging, advise her to make good choices on what she shares and how much time she spends on these things.

- If your teen works, take the opportunity to speak in a public setting about goals, roles, and other forms of behaving respectfully.

You can speak to your teen and help him prepare for complicated or unpleasant scenarios in advance. Discuss what he will do if he is in a group and someone takes drugs or is under pressure to have sex, or someone who has been drinking is given a trip. Respect the need for privacy from your teenager. Encourage the child to get enough sleep and exercise, and to eat safe, nutritious meals.

Conclusion

The parent-child relationship is the basis on which kids' personality relies. Kids learn from their parents and consider them as their first role models. If you are a parent and want to strengthen your bonding with your children, "Positive Parenting" is the best way to do so.

Parenting has different styles, including authoritative, authoritarian, permissive, and uninvolved. The un-involved parenting style ranks lowest of all styles, and the authoritative parenting style is considered best as it allows kids to do what they want with some boundaries. Knowing these all styles and then choosing the best will help you overcoming parenting difficulties you face.

Kids' moods change with time, and you may be parenting different personalities at a time. So, do not tackle every kid in the same way as they need various commands. Spend quality time, make good memories with them, go for some family walks and picnics, share your feelings, and develop confidence in your kids. Most of the time, lack of confidence and stress come from the parents' side besides other causes.

Keeping kids safe from molesters and other dangers are your first duty if you are a parent. Tell your child about sexual abuse and make them conscious of their body ownership and give them such confidence to share everything with you openly.

Whining is a behavior that children show to get what they want, but do not let it be their habit and use other ways to share their feelings with you. Always talk to your kids like a friend and observe them like a guardian. Be a calm parent and teach your kids to be obedient but not forcefully.

If you are a toddler parent and worry about managing your kid activities, or your kids are grown to teens and want to administer them, you can do it quickly. For all the age groups, there are positive parenting tips. These tips provide your kids' developmental milestones and provide your nutrition guide, health, and safety considerations. Choose to be a positive parent by adopting positive parenting tips and living a happy life with your little kids.

9 798737 647650